101 TRUE TALES FROM THE TERMINAL

Wild, Wacky & Wonderful Stories That'll Take You Away

An Anthology, Edited by Desiree Miller

Printed in the United States of America
First Printing, 2024

ISBN 979-8-89390-016-3

Library of Congress Control Number: Pending

Ordering Information: Special discounts are available on quantity purchases by bookstores, corporations, associations, and others. For details, contact the publisher at sales@braughlerbooks.com or at 937-58-BOOKS.

For questions or comments about this book, please write to sales@braughlerbooks.com

Dedication:

For my mother, Laura, forever the fan of a fun getaway and the person who inspired my travel addiction, and for my youngest child, Daly, who is always up for exploring a new corner of the world with me, and one of the few people I'm ok with suffering in the middle seat for so she can have the window.

Contents

101 True Tales from the Terminal

I used to play a game at the airport to help pass the time while waiting for my next flight. I'd watch people walk by and dream up stories about them. Who they are. Where they're going. It would start off innocently enough. The people all dressed up in suits or heels were clearly on their way to their job out of town, unless the heels were really high; they were likely on their way to see a man they wanted to impress. Maybe a boyfriend they hadn't seen in months, or possibly a lover who traded off flights each week, so they could 'connect' in whatever city of choice for that weekend. The moms with newborns sleeping in a sling were taking the baby to meet Grandma for the first time. The guys in uniform were off to their next deployment. I always added a little prayer for safety when I saw them. Other people were harder to read, so I made their stories more interesting. They were bank robbers on the run, looking for a quick escape. Or guys getting away to a bachelor's weekend with old buddies in Vegas. It was fun making up their stories, and it was irrelevant if I ever found out if I was right about them. But I've learned in recent years, I don't have to guess as often. That's because, for whatever reason, people now seem to think the airport is where they can let it all hang out. They're often oblivious to those around them. They're spilling intimate details with people on the other end of a call that they don't realize, or don't care, everyone around them can hear. Heck, often they're on speakerphone for the entire conversation. Or, they're in vacation mode, where the rules seem to be left behind with their day-to-day lives, and just feel free to share things with the world, even if they just met us two minutes ago. Oh, and the emotion of it all. They're sometimes frustrated, and eagerly sharing their anger over travel in general, with the gate agent who becomes the target of their fury. Or, they may be stoically holding back tears that sneak out of the corners of their eyes anyway, as they endure the worst week of their life, heading to a loved one's funeral. They may be a little drunk from hitting the bar during their delays. But most of the time, they're just funny. Often hysterical, actually. And the airport seems to bring out their most comedic side. Not intentionally. Nope. They may not even know they're funny, but they certainly have me laughing. The airport seems to bring out all the feels. Mad, sad, drunk, or just dopey. This book is full of stories about the crazy things travelers are doing, or seeing, while waiting for their next flight, or when they're in the air. They're all true, even if they seem hard to believe. I hope you enjoy these tales from the terminal, and beyond, and keep your eyes open for more the next time you're waiting for a plane. And if you see something you think others would love hearing about, send that story my way to 101TalesfromtheTerminal@gmail.com and maybe we'll be able to include it in the sequel I will write next, "More True Tales from the Terminal."

Until then, thanks for joining me on this trip!

Des

The Day That Started It All

ATL TO DAY

Atlanta, GA, to Dayton, OH, Oct. 2022

This book was inspired by a simple social media post, written up on an otherwise ordinary Wednesday morning, while I was seated at Atlanta's Hartsfield Jackson Airport, waiting to catch a flight to a comedy writers' workshop in Dayton, Ohio. I wasn't particularly excited to go, to be honest. As a travel writer, I was used to my destinations being a little more exotic than Dayton. Or Ohio, for that matter. But as a gal who rarely writes with humor, I was eager to "find my funny," no matter where the conference was happening. I didn't realize that I'd have a plan for an entire book about funny stuff before the workshops even started. Here's the post, and the catalyst for what's to follow.

"I love airports. I have only been sitting here about 30 minutes and haven't talked to a soul yet, but have already heard three different conversations about so much drama...one man who thought he hit the jackpot when he was offered $500 for his seat to Destin, Florida, 'til he called his mom who promptly told him to get on that flight and not make her wait to pick him up four hours later. Another man (who likes to speak on the speakerphone of his cell) missed his connecting flight because he left his phone on the last plane when it fell out of his coat pocket in the overhead compartment. He realized this at his new gate, so he had to go back to another terminal to the last plane to retrieve it. Luckily he got it, or unluckily for us listening to him call people and repeating the story. And there's a new mom beside me with her baby who now has more air miles in the last year than most of us...she was telling the gal sitting next to her just how much she hates this big airport with all of its trains and so much walking. Her home airport is apparently tiny. But she travels to see her mom who has cancer and pneumonia and I'm not sure what else. But the baby is a good flier, so there's that. I swear, I could sit here all day hearing all the stories. Airports are gold mines for them."

More than one friend told me there was a whole book in these fun interactions many of us seem to have while just going about our business at the airport. Unless you're the type to throw on earphones and go into your own zone, you're bound to hear something that'll make you laugh. And even if you can't hear it because of the earphones, you're likely to see something that'll give you a giggle or a grin. Or, in some cases, a full on belly laugh. Keep reading for more True Tales from the Terminal.

CHAPTER ONE

THE TICKET COUNTER

These days, we can avoid a lot of travel nightmares by booking flights and checking in online, saving our boarding pass to our phone. That way, the only reason we need to go to the airline ticket counter before we fly is to drop off a checked bag. Sounds simple, until it's not. For example, if you make a mistake with the ticket you booked, or if your checked bag is heavier than the weight limits allow, the ticketing agent can either be your best friend or your worst nightmare, and sometimes, that depends on your behavior while you're standing there.

A Wild Ride

(and We're Not Talking About the Flight)

BNA TO DEN

Nashville, TN, to Denver, CO, April 2024
Written by
Meredith Whitehead of Mer's Life (www.merslife.com)

While traveling home from a convention in Nashville, I snapped a cute little picture of my splayed luggage at the ticket counter with the intention of posting something like, "Not me, having to repack my entire bag because it was SEVENTEEN pounds over the weight limit from all the free swag I got!" to Facebook.

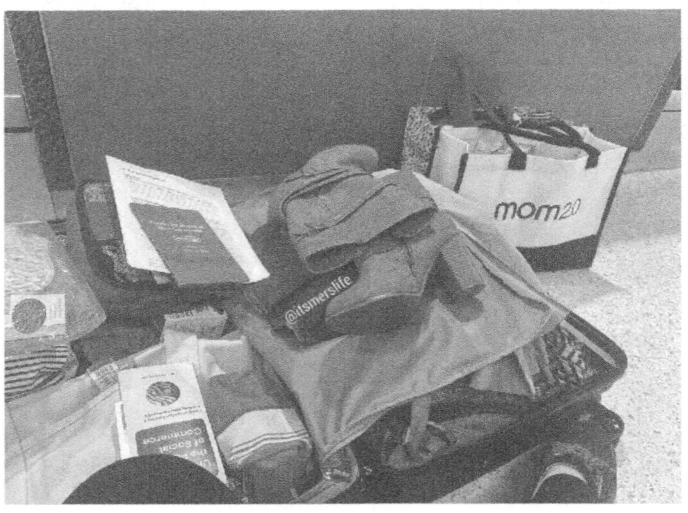

The contents of Meredith's overpacked suitcase

Hahahaha, joke's on me.

I grabbed one of several free totes out of my bag and started unloading anything free/heavy that I didn't arrive in Nashville with. Yay me for getting ALL the things at this conference. The Southwest employee helping me was super kind and even let me get away with a 56-pound bag because I told him my arms may actually fall off carrying all this shit through the airport. He slapped a "heavy load" or whatever sticker on that puppy and sent it down the chute.

As I walked away, I reached for my phone to make my cute lil' haha post, only I didn't HAVE my phone. I pinged it from my watch and listened carefully to the bags I was carrying - silence. So, I rushed back to the counter to see if I'd left it sitting there. The employee saw my panicked face and asked what was wrong? I told him that I must've set my phone down and now it's gone. He quickly determined it was probably IN my checked bag, which was already on its way to the plane. This sweet man offered to chase it down, but said that it would take him 15 to 20 minutes. I declined, not wanting to make his job more difficult. This was such a Meredith thing to do, so I figured that it was the universe telling me I needed a break from my phone for a few hours. He prints me another boarding pass because I am so scattered I can't find the one I just got, and I rush toward security.

Fast forward to me arriving at my gate and realizing my laptop was in one of my carry-on bags. I open it up to check the Track My Phone thingy and see where my phone is in-relation to my plane. Strangely enough, my phone was not close at all, but 6.6 miles AWAY and moving further and further from the airport. It's at this point that I realize, holy f*ck, someone has my phone. What kind of MONSTER?

I call my husband from my watch and tell him what is going on, in a total panic and almost crying. At this point, everyone around me at the gate is listening to my story (watch = speaker phone) and they are invested. Some people are telling me how to do an iCloud backup, some people are offering to drive to the address that my phone is showing, everyone is offering to help and incredibly kind. I quickly learned how to report my phone as lost and ping it with a message to call me when found. No more than a minute later, my phone goes offline. At this point, I'm 100% sure that someone stole my phone at baggage check and has turned it off so that it can't be tracked.

When we board the plane, I try to ping my phone once more and it is still out of range. Now the map tells me it's more than 8 miles away and still traveling. I'm f*cked. I spend the next three hours wanting to throw up. It's not even the stupid expensive phone, which IS insured, but an entire weekend of connections and work stored IN said phone. I don't utilize the cloud like I should (well NOW I do) so the last automatic backup had been the first morning of my conference, four days earlier.

Toward the end of my flight, I try to ping my bag once again to see, if by some miracle, it's within range and actually on this damn plane with me. The phone pings. Of course, I can't hear a thing, but my brain starts to spin. Is my phone actually in my bag and sitting 10 feet below me?

When we land in Denver, I'm literally running to baggage claim to find my bag and open it. It's the third one down the chute and I am AGGRESSIVE in my baggage retrieval. I set the bag down, press my ear to it, and ping my phone. "Ding ding ding da da ding ding ding!" Cut to me absolutely crying when I open my bag and find my phone under a pile of shit, along with my original boarding pass.

Phew, what a stupid, wild ride.

One Little Letter Makes All the Difference

SJO, SJU, SJC

and more
San Jose and San Juan

It's really easy to make major mistakes when you're booking flights.

Expensive mistakes, too.

I once had a conference I needed to attend in Costa Rica, and was a millisecond away from booking my flight into San Jose, super proud of myself when I found an airfare for significantly less than my friends who were also going to this conference. I love saving money, so I was eager to share my great lower rate with my travel buddies. It was one of those friends who quickly pointed out it was no deal; it was, in fact, a rate for a different flight, to a different country!

Oof!

I was trying to get to SJO, in San Jose, Costa Rica. But I was looking at rates to SJU. THAT airport is San Juan, Puerto Rico.

I can see me now, landing in the wrong country! Or even worse, having to buy a sky-high ticket to the RIGHT country at the airport on the same day!

Later, when I mentioned to another friend how close I came to booking the wrong flight, she told me not to feel bad; she actually HAD made that error, except she mistakenly bought a flight to SJC, which is San Jose, CALIFORNIA!

One little letter difference can really cost you!

It turns out lots of people make similar mistakes, though, not just in the airport code letters, but mixing up times, too.

Fellow travelers shared these expensive errors from their journeys:

"I missed my connecting flight in Finland all because I didn't realize there was a time difference between Finland and Norway." This man told me he had to stay an extra night in Helsinki, which cost him 150 bucks.

It was a much more expensive error for this dad of four, who flew his family to the wrong island in the Bahamas. He explained, "We landed in the Bahamas and walked out of the airport and asked the taxi driver to take us to our resort." His response? "You're on the wrong island." He had to take his family back to the airport to take a regional airline to the next island over on a tiny plane.

It even happens to pilots, as David Baker shared. "I was flying to a small town on the Tennessee/Virginia border in 1995, traveling to meet a client. I landed in the wrong town, tied the plane down, and was walking to the FBO (what a terminal is called in a small airport) with my luggage and saw the sign and realized my mistake. Bristol, TN vs. Bristol, VA." Even more fun was when he WAS looking in the right state, but the city's airport is actually not in the same state you'd think. He shares, "I was flying an instrument flight plan in very bad weather, and I'd been cleared for an approach to land in Cincinnati. I started flipping through my leather-bound instrument landing charts, going to OHIO and looking for that city. It was nowhere to be found, and I was panicking. After a long pause, the air traffic controller said, "Try looking under Kentucky." He'd seen this before. The airport isn't actually in Ohio."

One commercial pilot even LANDED at the wrong airport once. It was a Piedmont Airlines flight in 1986, where the pilot confused smaller Daniel Field for the larger Bush Field airport in Augusta, Georgia. The big passenger plane was on the wrong and much smaller runway, which made for a rough landing. The passengers had to wait to get off because there were no stairs tall enough for them, and then they had to be bussed to the correct airport for their connecting flights and bags.

Sometimes, it's not about going to the wrong PLACE, but the wrong TIME. It happens to many people who struggle with converting military time, or just misread the time, like this man who told me about the flight he missed. "I read 17:45 as 7:45 pm. The people at the counter at Newark were packing up & going home when I showed up to check in!" Another person shared, in response, "Same! I read 18:45 as 8:45 pm and yup, missed the flight." And yet another man jumped into that conversation, acknowledging, "I made the same mistake for a flight from Philadelphia to London. For a family of 4. $1000 worth of change fees got us on a flight the next day. Had to ride the train back home. Now I obsessively check tickets for 24 hour time."

Of course, as with all things in life, how you react may change everything.

That was the case for another fellow who told me he missed his connecting flight, but it actually worked out for the best. He explained, "When I realized I'd have to stay overnight, I started to lay into the airline worker, then stopped myself." It hit him that this worker probably got grief all day long from others, so he took a different approach. He apologized and asked what he could do. Ultimately, he took a shuttle to a hotel, stayed overnight, and went back to the airport the next day. He explained, "When we checked in, the airline worker remembered me and gave me and my son first class tickets for our flight to England. It was amazing. We'd never flown first class before."

It's true, the airport staff can make or break your trip, so it definitely can pay to be kind.

Just a reminder, before you hit that purchase button, double-check yourself, and maybe call a friend to confirm you're headed to the right country, at the right time, too.

CHAPTER TWO

PUT ALL PERSONAL BELONGINGS IN THE PLASTIC CONTAINER

We've all heard the commands as you approach security:

Remove your shoes, belt and jacket, and take everything out of your pockets (unless you're fortunate enough to have TSA Precheck, in which case, you get the golden ticket to just take the stuff out of your pockets). Throw away your food and liquids, and follow single file through the body scanner.

But sometimes, things don't exactly go as planned when you weave your way through security, as we hear from the following flyers.

Is That Cake in Your Bag, or Are You Happy to See Me?

CLT TO LGA

Charlotte, North Carolina, to
New York City, New York, 1991
By Leslie Duffield

For a small town girl, a trip to New York City is a big deal. Especially when it's for a bachelorette party with a bunch of women who actually LIVE in New York City!

It was the early 90's, so air travel was far less restrictive. I was traveling with the bride-to-be from Charlotte, North Carolina, to "The Big Apple". We were meeting several of her friends, and staying at an apartment overlooking Central Park. Everything was new and exciting to me, from the cab rides, to the bar scene, to the Broadway play we saw. But the icing on the cake, literally, was the bachelorette party cake from an X-rated bakery. I mean, who even knew that was a thing!

On top of this beautiful pink and white bridal cake sat a giant, very detailed flesh-colored penis made of frosting. It was certainly the highlight of the party, and no one was willing to take a bite of that thing.

So naturally, we decided to take it home to Charlotte. We gently wrapped it up and put it in the future bride's carry-on bag. It was quickly forgotten as we left for the airport bleary-eyed and hungover.

It wasn't until we heard several people laughing and pointing – both employees and passengers – that we realized the giant penis was clearly visible on the security screener's x-ray machines – for all to see!

It looked like the mother of all sex toys going across the screen!

All we could do was laugh, too, grab the bag and go. And of course, several of those who witnessed the whole thing, were of course on our same flight!

Bringing Family Along

HLN TO BZE

Helena, Montana, to Belize
Shared by
Lydia of Helena, MT

It's always nice to take family to places they've never been before. But in Lydia's case, the family trip had a twist.

My husband and I were on our way to Belize, and took the ashes of my father, brother-in-law, and cousin. None of them had the chance to go there when they were alive, so we just put their ashes in three separate plastic baggies, thinking they'd like to have a little bit of a resting place down there in the sun and sand.

When we got to the TSA, the agent asked us what was in the baggies.

My husband: "The ashes of our brother, father, and cousin. Sorry, we left their passports at home."

I thought the agent was going to die laughing when he heard that (pun not intended).

Granted, they still tested the outside for explosives.

Finding none, they sent us on our way.

All five of them, off to the sunshine and sand of Belize, where three got to stay forever.

Criminal or Kind Old Lady?

TPA TO EWR

Tampa, FL, to Newark, New Jersey, 2005 ish
Shared by
Lisa Parker about her mother, Patricia Maleski

There are few people on this planet kinder than my Aunt Patty.

She spent decades as a nurse, volunteered with countless charities, and, in what mattered to me most as a little girl lucky enough to call her my aunt, she never forgot a birthday. Ever. She really lived to make others feel loved and cared for, and I can't recall a time I heard her say or do anything but be kind.

But the folks at security at the Tampa, FL, airport didn't know my Aunt Patty.

They just knew there was a woman who'd gone through security that afternoon, headed to Newark, New Jersey, with a weapon in her purse, and who knew WHAT she was going to do with it?!

To tell this story properly, though, I need to back up a bit.

My aunt worked at a hospital in Clearwater, Florida, for many years. It was a colleague's birthday on this day, and she, true to her nature, was bringing in a coffee cake to make sure this person knew they deserved to be celebrated. She threw a knife in her purse to make sure they had a way to cut it into pieces, and then went about her business of the day. Her work family huddled for a little party, sang the song and ate the cake, and after Patricia cleaned up and washed the utensils, she threw the knife right back into her bag, where she promptly forgot about it the rest of the day.

After all, she had a busy afternoon ahead. She had a flight with her husband, Lou, early that evening, to go see their daughter and two beautiful grandchildren. She just had to finish out the work day, head on out to the airport, and be on their merry way.

After making this trip enough times, she and her hubby were travel professionals, always just bringing a carry-on bag and her purse. So, when they got to the airport, that's what they brought through security.

Uncle Lou, always the gentleman, let his wife go first, as he followed.

And that's where things go awry, quickly.

TSA scanners spot the knife and start freaking out.

"Is this your bag?", they demand an answer.

She's startled but tells them yes.

"So, this is your knife?" they follow up.

The horror of her mistake hits her.

She's frazzled and tries to explain, "Oh, but it was my friend's birthday, and we had to cut the cake!"

The TSA agents don't want to hear it. They start dragging her away, in tears.

Lou is also upset, but they're keeping him separate, telling him to take his bag and move beyond the security zone. They won't let him near her. He's desperate, not sure how to help her without getting himself arrested, too, assuming they're in the midst of reading his precious Patricia her rights as he's standing there.

Meanwhile, in a private holding room, agents are going through all of her stuff, giving her the third degree on WHERE she's going, WHY she's going there, and what her plan is once she gets there.

But she's my sweet Aunt Patty, and they start to realize she's no criminal.

Ultimately, they accept that she really is just a 'cute old lady' with the very best of intentions, so they let her go, upset and embarrassed, but free to continue on her journey to see her daughter, and to keep doing nice things for others in life, just maybe without the steak knife in the future.

Big Birtha

(not Bertha, but Birtha)

DAY TO DEN

Dayton, Ohio, to Denver, Colorado, 2017

By

Rajean Blomquist

"Ma'am, please step aside."

A phrase you might be excited about if it is to count your winnings from the slot machine spitting out a bucket of coins.

Not so much as you are going through the x-ray scanner in the security line at the airport.

"Do you want a male or a female agent to frisk you?"

Hmm. It depends on the frisk.

I asked why?

"Ma'am you have a large package showing on x-ray between your legs."

What?! I wasn't traveling with my husband.

He showed me the image. That sucker could have been my carry-on bag. Well, I suppose in a sense it WAS my carry-on. I couldn't get mad if they charged me extra baggage fees.

Not gonna lie, I knew something was askew. Women talk a lot about a lot of things, but in general we don't talk about bladder leakage. We know it happens, we see the commercials, but we don't go into personal detail.

I had been sprinting to the bathroom for about a year. I had perfected the pee pee dance, which was worthy of the mirror ball trophy on *Dancing with the Stars*. The steel trap bladder I sported in my youth was gone.

After my TSA pat down, I researched and found a female surgeon whose office walls were lined with her overachievements. Peace Corp, awards, she speaks four languages, and she was a Girl Scout. That was important because I wanted someone who could tie a mean four point knot.

Tests revealed the issue was not my bladder - though that was along for the ride. That misplaced surprise on the x-ray was my uterus!

I named my uterus Birtha, unconventional spelling, I know, but this fits the purpose of the body organ. She served me well, but I don't miss her hanging around. Literally.

Hanging around. Hanging down. The clinical term is prolapsed. Birtha was stage 4. That's end stage. End stage in this sense is near your knees.

Birtha is now gone. Removed. Extracted, thanks to an urgently scheduled hysterectomy that ended up taking much longer than scheduled.

While I'm super thankful this medical diagnosis didn't turn out to be terminal, I'm happy the agent in the airport terminal had his eagle eyes focused on the prize. Embarrassing as it was at the time of discovery, it's now my favorite travel story about lost and found baggage. Normally, you don't celebrate your TSA pat down at the airport, but I'm happy the heightened security measures forced me to more fully investigate my medical mystery and bid good old Birtha farewell.

Next time you see someone pulled out of line at the security checkpoint, perhaps you can have more empathy for them. They may not be trying to smuggle contraband. Their uterus or other pieces or parts in their nether regions simply may not be neatly stored in their upright position.

Airport Stampede

ATL

Atlanta, GA, November 2021
Shared by
Howard Kramer

Travel days around Thanksgiving can be the busiest, and by default, often the craziest, but few people were expecting the disarray that took place at Atlanta's Hartsfield Jackson Airport on the Saturday before Thanksgiving in 2021. This is Howard Kramer's story on that day that went from calm to chaos in seconds.

I had just made my way through security, and was waiting at the T-gate, the terminal closest to the security screening area. I was sitting at a restaurant, enjoying a slice of pizza and scrolling on my phone, when I heard a sudden rumbling sound. It got louder and louder and it hit me, I'd heard that noise before. It was the sound of a stampede, and I knew not to throw myself into the crowd, but to move instead to the back of the restaurant, behind the counter.

It was from there I saw the first wave of the stampede driving past, with about 50 people trying to duck into the restaurant's restrooms. Others stood off to the side while still others joined me, ducking down behind the counter. Someone yelled that there was a shooter at security, and my adrenaline started to kick in.

Another wave of people stampeded by, heading to the far end of the terminal, and some security guards were yelling for them to run; to leave their bags where they were and go, fast! A calmer guard rushed in and said there was an active shooter in security, and told us all to get out, and hurriedly escorted us to a side exit to leave the airport terminal.

Several of us ran across the street to a parking structure, where we hid behind a low wall, and stayed for more than an hour, maybe longer. Because no shooter had been caught, the airport was in a lockdown of sorts, until ultimately people felt it was safe enough to start walking around. Who knows how much time had passed.

Flights that had been delayed were getting back on track and security was working through the chaos of trying to get people back through, despite the fact they'd left much of their luggage and identification in the terminal on the other side. It was a challenge, to say the least.

A few people had been injured in the stampede. Many had missed or rescheduled flights on one of the worst travel times for such an incident to happen. Fortunately, the worst of it for me, once my adrenaline stopped pumping, was that my dad ended up waiting hours for me at the airport I was flying into.

It would be days before the shooter was caught. And it all turned out to be a massive mistake. The man's bag had been flagged by machines at security for a closer look, and when that happened, the gun owner reached in and the gun went off, inside the bag, by all accounts an accident. No one was shot, but the sound was enough to set off a panic. The gun owner was able to run and blend in with passengers racing out in the chaos, but he was ultimately caught and charged. And Atlanta airport security crews had quite the drill, though you can bet they wished it had been just that, a drill.

Giddy Up!

LAX TO BDL

Los Angeles, California, to Bradley
International Airport, Hartford, Connecticut, 2004
Shared by
Stacey Owens

Have you ever tried to travel with a whip, saddle and spurs?

In a car, that's no big deal.

But getting them on an airplane, in your carry-on bags? That's another matter entirely. Just ask Stacey Owens, who admits, it wasn't easy, but then again, this wasn't her first rodeo.

When I was in college at Mount Holyoke in Massachusetts, I was part of an equestrian team. So, when I went back and forth from my Los Angeles home to college during school breaks, I took my expensive gear, or my 'tack' if we're using proper horse lingo, along with me. The saddle itself was thousands of dollars, and not the kind of thing I wanted in a suitcase that would likely be tossed around on airport conveyor belts and the like. And I definitely didn't want it lost if my baggage never arrived. So, I put it in its travel bag, then threw my helmet, whip and spurs in my backpack I always brought with me.

I checked in for my flight in L.A. and headed to the security lines. I put my gear on the conveyor belt to go through the scanners. And in a flash, I was being ordered to a back room, security surrounding me.

I watched as they wheeled in a cart with my backpack.

"Can you tell us about your stuff?" they ask.

"What would you like to know?" I respond. And before I go any further, please know I 100% admit I'm a bit of a smart aleck, especially when dealing with people who are aggravating me.

"What is it? Why are you traveling with it?" they want to know.

I explain I ride horses. I tell them I ride for my school team. Then I tell them what I think looks obvious, that this is my saddle, this is my whip, and these are my spurs.

"Why do you need this on a plane?"

"I carry it with me, so it won't get damaged in cargo," I tell them.

"Well, you have a weapon," they say.

I'm stumped. I'm wondering if maybe I left my nail clippers in my bag, or a pair of scissors or something. I'm clearly confused, so they tell me to open my backpack.

I follow the order and pull out my spurs.

Bingo! They tell me those are weapons.

I say no, they're not. They're spurs. They're used for horses, not weapons. And sure, they may have a sharp point, but it'd be really tough to hurt someone with their hexagon shape. I continue, "They're considered safe by the Federation Equestrian International (FEI), so why wouldn't they be acceptable to fly with?"

They respond with, "Because you can hurt someone."

They don't love this next part, but I reply with, "You can hurt someone with a pencil."

Yeah, that doesn't go over well at all.

I explain I've flown with them before and don't see the issue, and they tell me they need to get their manager, the *head of security.

I wait and start getting concerned I'm going to miss my flight.

The manager walks in and appears startled that he's dealing with a 20-something year old, not an older person being difficult.

I repeat the ordeal I JUST went through with the other security agents.

Then I look at my watch.

"Do you have somewhere to be?" he asks me.

"Yes, on a plane."

I follow that up with the urgency of my impending flight, having already spent about an hour and a half in the room, and the fact that I just want to get back to school.

He wants to know why I didn't check the saddle, to which I explain, it's a five-thousand dollar piece of equipment, and unless he wants to be liable if it's damaged or lost, I'm keeping it. He then tells me he needs to keep the spurs. Quickly, I let him know if he needs them, he'll have to pay me for them, because they're hard to replace.

He finally relents, telling me, "You have to promise me you won't hurt anyone with them."

My reply, "...unless I'm provoked."

Somehow, I'm miraculously cleared and fortunately, no one provoked me on the plane, so I can stay true to my promise.

For the record, spurs are allowed on a plane, in both checked bags and carry-on. But if you're wearing them, you'll need to take them off to get through security. I don't attempt to wear them.

To this day, I don't understand why they didn't consider the whip the weapon to be most concerned about, since that could likely do a lot more damage, on a flight or on the ground. That said, whips are also on the TSA's approved list, just in case you need to bring one along on your next trip, for horses or some other hobby.

A Very Unique Souvenir

MSY TO BOS

New Orleans, Louisiana, to
Boston, Massachusetts
Shared by
Niri Kumar

Lots of us like to pick up souvenirs on our travels. I like to get an ornament, or a unique piece of jewelry, from each place I visit. Other people buy magnets.

When Niri Kumar went on a trip to New Orleans, she decided to bring back a taste of the town and bought a box of beignet mix to take home with her.

It turns out airport security isn't a fan of powders in boxes, so when she was going through the security line, they quickly pulled her aside. I'll let her take it from there.

I didn't know the lady behind me in line, but she was pulled out, too, for another security risk.

I've learned it's best in life if I try not to rock the boat, but this lady was not happy, and she made it very clear.

Young, irritated, and annoyed, she said she had no time for such nonsense. She didn't appreciate being pulled into a separate area of security, along with me, to answer questions about whatever had alerted security.

Even though I was before her in line, the woman created such a scene about needing to leave, the TSA agents helped her first. As much as I wanted to get out of there, I wasn't looking to argue with anyone who could keep me from my flight home.

So I sat quietly, observing them as they questioned her and watch them pull a massive bullet from her carry-on. Like gigantic. Big enough to fit across her entire palm when she held it. I'm talking a mini-missile.

The security agents tell the woman she can't take a live round of ammunition on a plane. This was not a simple shell. It was not a spent bullet.

She insists, of course she can; "It's cute," she says, just a souvenir she decided to bring back.

"No ma'am, you can't," they tell her.

This goes back and forth, but ultimately, the TSA wins, every time.

They send her on her way, but keep her big bullet.

My box of beignet powder looks less lethal by the minute, and I get to keep it as I head for my flight.

Those magnets are looking like better and better souvenirs, right?

PB&J

ATL TO JNB

Atlanta, Georgia, to
Johannesburg, South Africa, June 2022
Shared by
Shanon Pretorius

Peanut butter and jelly.

It's about as tame as it gets when it comes to a go-to meal. So it may shock you that the TSA may disagree.

Just ask Shanon Pretorius, who shared her run-in with the TSA with me.

"My husband Andrew and I were traveling to Johannesburg, South Africa, to visit family. Andrew has an autoimmune disease called EOE, which is triggered by eating any type of dairy. This tends to make traveling and eating out a bit difficult. We knew we were looking at a 16-hour flight, and the airline serves meals, but we wanted to be on the safe side and pack food from home just in case. So what's the easiest meal we could bring with us? PB&J obviously. That morning we made four PB&J sandwiches, each in individual sandwich bags, and then in Tupperware. We checked a bag and both had carry-ons. Andrew's bag immediately got flagged and pulled as we went through TSA. Neither of us was sure what he could have packed that wouldn't be allowed through security. We see the agent pull out the Tupperware full of sandwiches. It's funny, because of course the only thing he can eat is potentially about to get thrown away. Instead, the agent takes each PB&J out of the box and proceeds to inspect each one. Thankfully, they left the sandwiches in the bags during the inspection, but they did pull them apart in the bag. Our sandwiches were eventually deemed safe, though we did receive some slightly judgmental comments and looks from the agent."

*Side note: As crazy as it sounds, the agent was generous to allow it through, because peanut butter *is considered a liquid by the TSA. Seriously. And they've gotten a whole lot of grief from fliers for saying so. TSA defines a liquid as something which "has no definite shape and takes a shape dedicated by its container." Well, there you go. And, because it's a liquid, you can only bring 3.4 ounces or less in your carry-on. Odds are Shanon and Andrew probably had that much spread on each of the four sandwiches.*

But it's a lucky thing the security agent let it pass, because, once on board, the duo discovered the meals on the flight were in fact, NOT dairy-free, despite the airline being made aware of his allergy. That would have been a LONG flight without any food.

As Shanon said, "PB&J sandwiches for the win!"

First Class Delivery

(A sweet thank you note)

Shared by a friend who is a flight attendant (who asked to remain anonymous), but didn't want a new family to stress throughout their flight about what they could feed their baby.

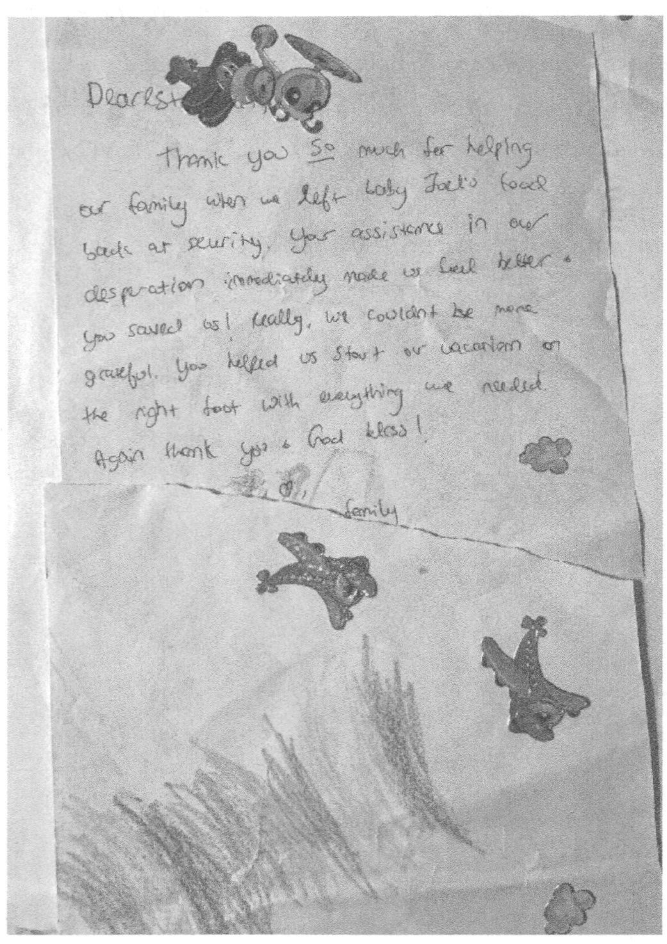

Dearest

Thank you so much for helping
our family when we left baby Jack's food
back at security. Your assistance in our
desperation immediately made us feel better &
you saved us! Really, we couldn't be more
grateful. You helped us start our vacation on
the right foot with everything we needed.
Again thank you & God bless!

Family

These days, it's tough to know which items you pack will make it through security, but the rules tend to feel more relaxed if you're flying with a baby. However, when one couple, traveling with a baby and a toddler, had to turn over their baby's food after it was deemed a security risk, they weren't sure what they were going to do about feeding him later, on their hours-long flight.

They didn't realize they had one of the world's best flight attendants (my words, not hers) on the plane they later boarded. I'll let my flight attendant friend take it from here.

This couple was distraught, and it showed, so I asked what was wrong, and if there was some way I could help.

The young parents explained that "Baby Joel's" food was taken at security, and they were desperate, trying to figure out a solution for their infant who wasn't quite ready for the real food the airline would be serving on the flight.

The plane was still boarding, and I knew I had a tiny window where I could do something to help them. I couldn't leave the plane, because of my responsibilities getting the other passengers seated and settled, but I could go ask one of the pilots if they might be able to do something, which is what I did.

I shared their story, and the sympathetic co-pilot decided he could make this better, leaving the plane and rushing back to the security area, where he asked the supervisor if he could retrieve the baby food that had been confiscated from the family not long before. You see, pilots can go through with things the rest of us can't, so the security agent handed over the food and the pilot raced back to his plane.

The young couple was overjoyed that we pulled off a mini-miracle to help their child, so they decided they needed to do some small favor in return. During the flight, they wrote a sweet thank you note, complete with scribbles and stickers of airplanes from their toddler's prized collection. It read:

Thank you so much for helping our family when we left baby Joel's food at security. Your assistance in our desperation immediately made us feel better. You helped save us. Thank you, and God bless.

And they didn't just give the letter to me, they sent it to my bosses.

We might have helped feed the baby's belly, but their thank you letter fed my heart, knowing sometimes the extra effort really does make a difference.

What's in a Name?

CTE TO ATL

Cartagena, Columbia, to Atlanta, Georgia
Shared by
Joe Hernandez

If you've flown in the past two decades, you're likely aware of the No Fly List put together by the U.S. Government. It's a list of people no longer allowed to board an airplane, and was created after 9/11, with national security as its main objective. The government can put people on the list, or take them off, for a variety of reasons, and if your name ends up on it, no one has to tell you why. They can keep the reason and the evidence secret if they choose. They're supposed to send you a letter letting you know, but there's always a chance you might still be pulled from the security line because your name was flagged. If you have a common name, or share your name with a bad guy, it's possible you aren't even the same person they are blocking, but you'll have to prove that.

That's something that happened to my friend, Joe Hernandez, all the time, as he explains here.

Years ago, I used to get stopped every time I came through immigration since I have a very common Hispanic last name. For some reason, I always get stopped in Cartagena, Colombia, when traveling for business. On a few of my international work trips I went with my coworker and friend Peter Jones (may he rest in peace), whose name was apparently shared with a good number of criminals. On a few of those occasions when I thought I was definitely going to be stopped, I was somehow spared the extra questioning, and saw how Peter was sent to the 'room' to answer questions before being let in the country. One time, as we were in the line at immigration with a couple of coworkers, I jokingly told him to let me get ahead of him in line, since he was inevitably going to be stopped and I didn't want to be held back by him being delayed, and he laughed, telling me that this time I was definitely the one getting stopped. But I wasn't, and he was again delayed and sent to the 'room'. We had a laugh after he finally was let in the country after a little over an hour.

I guess you never know. And I also guess you should be very careful who you choose to travel with. As for Joe, he now has Global Entry, so he breezes through U.S. Immigration, problem-free.

Arrested and Propositioned

Miami, Florida, 1976
Shared by
Robin Dohrn-Simpson

My sister was a Rotary Exchange student to Brazil in 1975. She arranged for the son of a family in Brasilia to come to the US and stay with my family, and for me to go live with his family. After I graduated from high school in 1975, I headed down to Brazil. I lived there for around 3 years, went to the Universidade Católica de Goiás, taught English at an English school, made many friends and traveled extensively throughout Brazil, Paraguay, Uruguay and Argentina.

When I was forced by the Immigration Department to leave the country for at least 6 months before I could reapply for a student visa, I decided to return to the USA.

I booked my ticket and arranged stops in Manaus, Bogota and Caracas, before entering back into the USA via Miami.

I said goodbye to my many friends and the families that I had lived with, packed a HUGE suitcase that took me days to pack just so, in order to get everything in it that I had purchased over the years and began my journey home.

When I was in Bogota, my purse was slashed open from the bottom and my wallet, passport and airline ticket were stolen. I chased the thief through the nasty streets of the slums of Bogota but was not able to catch him. Fortunately, I had left my money in the safe at the hotel, but I didn't have any identification with me.

I went to the embassy and asked what I should do. They told me I didn't have enough time to get another passport, since my flight out was in a day or two. They recommended that I return through Miami and tell the officers the story, and hopefully they'd let me through customs.

Remember, this was the time of lots of drugs being transported through Venezuela and Colombia to the USA; the beginning of the 'War on Drugs.'

When I arrived in Miami and told the customs officers of my situation, they immediately arrested me and brought me to a questioning room, along with my HUGE suitcase. There I was, held by a customs official who, for it seemed like hours, questioned and requestioned me, as he went through everything in my suitcase. He even tested my shampoo and conditioner for drugs. He pulled everything out of my suitcase willy-nilly, and then suggested that I re-pack it. (Being the stubborn Taurus that I am, I suggested he re-pack it, as it took me weeks to pack that suitcase.) He just looked at me like I was a petulant girl. So, needless to say, I spent the next hour trying to squeeze everything back into that suitcase.

After I was cleared, he suggested that I book myself at the Airport Hotel, which I did.

Then, about an hour or so later, he called my room and asked me out on a date!

Claiming fatigue, I declined. To this day, I think about the audacity of that man!

How Can I Take Your Money Today?

NBO TO CAI

Nairobi, Kenya, to Cairo, Egypt, 2024
Shared by
Austin Stouffer

You never know whether you'll love a city on your bucket list until you get there, and sadly, sometimes, it's more of a nightmare than a dream. But you have to go to know, right? I'll let Austin elaborate.

20 countries in under 12 months.

That's how long and how many countries my wife and I are seeing on our world tour.

When we were one month in, we were flying from Nairobi, Kenya to Cairo, Egypt.

As we went through customs, I knew I was carrying a drone and Egypt was one of the countries where it wasn't allowed, so I declared it at customs, thinking they'd let me store it, just as I'd done weeks before in Kenya.

But I was wrong. Very wrong.

As soon as I told them about the drone, multiple security guards came over and started searching our bags, threatening to take our camera and other items that were obviously not an issue.

They then separated me and my wife, and took me in the back of the house (the part of the airport you never want to see).

They would not let me use my phone and they were only speaking Arabic to me and each other, so I had NO idea what was going on, and my wife was terrified.

They had me sitting in hallways, never explaining why.

After two hours, and my wife in tears at customs threatening to call the U.S. embassy, they finally walked me back out to meet her, but not before I was taken to a back stairwell. That's where the security guard used his phone's Google translator to tell me I had to pay him for his time.

I was in shock.

Ultimately, we were allowed to leave the airport.

And in the end, they put my drone in storage, exactly as I wanted.

There was no purpose to any of the run around, and it made a terrible first impression of the country, since it was the most terrifying experience of my life. And my wife's.

Ultimately, we cut our time in Egypt shorter than we'd planned, staying just five days.

Seeing the pyramids was really neat, but we felt like everywhere we went we were being gouged or extorted.

Even the street vendor said, and I quote, "How can I take your money today?"

And that pretty much summed up our visit perfectly.

Illicit Imports: Italian Meat and the Beagle Who Blew It

CTA TO FCO TO CLT TO ROA

Sicily, Italy, to Rome, Italy, to Charlotte, North Carolina, to Roanoke, Virginia, 2016

By E.B.

Ah, Italy.

The land of my birth, but better known as the land of delectable, delicious, divine food.

I'd taken my family on a vacation to see my birthplace, and we enjoyed gorging ourselves on all the gelato, prosciutto, pancetta, salami, and all the other appetizing treats the country has to offer. Fortunately, the daily marathons of walking everywhere we went, swimming and other fun was keeping us from packing on the pounds. But as our vacation came to an end, we decided we didn't want the daily gastronomic ecstasy to be over, too. So we asked ourselves, "Is it possible to bring some of this fun food home? I mean some of these $7 bottles of wine are all that I will ever need in our collection." And the cheese, oh my. Is Guanciale meat or cheese?

Burrata, mascarpone, mozzarella, fontina, gorgonzola, Taleggio, pecorino, provolone, ricotta, stracciatella, Grana Padano, parmigiano! How could we leave any of it behind?

So, we came up with a plan to bring the tastes of Italy to our home in Virginia.

But what are the rules for that?

Rules? No rules, we decided. Let's buy a suitcase and fill it with meat, cheese, and wine, and bring it all home.

In a normal relationship, the husband or wife would stop the other from their crazy ideas.

That's not the way we work, we are partners in crime. My wife simply said, "Great idea, how big a suitcase?"

We plotted our strategy:

Buy very big suitcase

Fill with meat, cheese, wine and other contraband

Cover with dirty laundry

Plead ignorance

So, off we went from Catania, Sicily, through Rome, to Charlotte, NC, with the ultimate goal of our home town of Roanoke, Virginia.

Catania was loud, crowded, and full of Sicilians.

I was showing my passport. In Italy, when the locals see that I am a fellow countryman, they regale me with a shower of really fast Italian. I spent most of my life in America, and my Italian is about as good as my packing ability, in need of a little more organization and practice. "Rallenta, per favore," is my go-to phrase, translated to "Please slow down."

We somehow got the luggage through Sicilian security, and are well on our way to being food smugglers. Even Rome was uneventful. We enjoyed a Peroni or two and incredible airport pizza (yes, in Rome it really is incredible), and we were on our way to Charlotte.

But upon deplaning, we started the long walk through what is basically a series of cattle chutes, testing even the most seasoned of travelers. "This way, move." Moo, moo moo, Americans here, everybody else here. Get your luggage and recheck through domestic travel.

They asked, "Are you carrying anything you shouldn't?" as we headed through customs and immigration.

"Nope not us," all good here we told 'em.

"Sir, you smell like a hot vat of cheese," they said. My response was that it had been a long day of travel and I hadn't showered for two days, plus I'd been eating cheese for the last three weeks, which must be why my skin was so shiny. They bought it and passed us through.

But then we had to recheck our bags for our final flight home.

A security lady with a really cute beagle was making her way through all of the travelers. This was odd, since we were already through. I tried not to make eye contact, but she kept coming. She was 80 feet away, then 60, then 20. She seemed very friendly and the dog just wasn't as intimidating as a large German Shepherd, so I relaxed. A little. Still, I tried to look distracted. I coughed, looked away, pretended to be on the phone. It didn't work. Ultimately, she and the beagle ended up standing right next to our suitcase.

"Hello, sir," she says to me, then continues, "We are training our new service dog. Can we please inspect your luggage?" I tried my best Italian, "Rallena for favor!" My wife looks at me like I'm an idiot and says, "Sure, which bags?"

The nice officer said all of them.

In my mind, I'm already busted. I'm processing as quickly as I can which family member who's an attorney I'm going to call. Will there be jail time? More importantly, will they take our meats and cheeses? Can we please keep the wine?

Should I just run for it? How about a bribe...look ma'am, I've got salami that will make you taller, proud to be alive and will just generally make your day go better.

But I keep quiet and hope this puppy is not as good a sniffer as she is cute.

We laid down suitcase one, opened it and the beagle thankfully wasn't interested.

We open suitcase two and have to pull out a diving mask and speargun. The officer loved the speargun and the beagle really loved the smell (there was a hint of octopus and fish still on the tip). No issue with suitcase three. But when we opened suitcase four, the Super Sleuth Beagle literally jumped into the middle and started digging. She emerged with a pair of my dirty shorts in her mouth, shaking it side to side.

I'm thinking to myself, it's over, we are gonna get it! This beagle is going to make the news: Beagle finds largest load of meat and cheese ever in North Carolina! But the officer responded by yelling, "No! No! Bad dog! Heel! Sit NO! Drop it!"

The officer then picked up the poor, sheepish beagle and set her down outside of the suitcase. People are starting to stare.

The beagle's head is low, and she looks ashamed, and the officer begins apologizing to me and my wife, both of us amazed. The officer explains, "I am so sorry. She is not supposed to do that and knows better. She has been trained to behave much better than that! Looks like she needs to go back to basic search training! Did she tear your shorts?"

Well, come to think of it, I want to say, but my wife reads my mind, looks at me again like I'm an idiot, and says no, his shorts are fine. She jokes with the officer, "I'm more worried about the health issues your poor puppy is going to have because she had them in her mouth!" The officer thought this was hilarious. She and my wife had a good laugh while I politely chuckled and thought health issue? They are not thaaaat dirty!

As the officer said her goodbyes and made a parting shot of "Get those shorts washed," I made brief eye contact with the cute beagle. It still haunts me today. Her eyes said, "You know that I know! I eyed her back and said I know that you know, and I am soooooo sorry. I hope basic beagle training is not that bad!"

We repacked, closed our suitcases and made our way through security and back home to Roanoke. Upon arriving home I washed my shorts, we toasted the cute beagle and ate like emperors for the next few months.

I hope that beagle made it through her training and is living her best life, to this day I still feel guilty for not fessing up.

CHAPTER THREE

WAITING TO BOARD

You've managed to book the right flight, to the right airport, and made it through security in one piece. Now you just have to get to your gate and wait to board. This is where things can start to get really interesting, as you trickle (or race, depending on how late you are) into the gate area, where your fellow passengers start filing in, too. You're united by the common hope that the flight is not delayed, or canceled, and that they actually have enough seats on your flight for you to be able to board. From here you may connect with someone who drives you nuts for the next several hours, or becomes one of your very best friends for life. Both are possible, which you'll see as you keep reading.

Now Boarding

(Everyone but You)

LAX TO FLL

Los Angeles, California, to
Ft. Lauderdale, Florida, November 2021
Written by
January Gordon Ornellas

Whenever I book a flight, I always end up in Group 7.

Even when I check in 24 hours ahead of time, ON THE DOT!

Tappity-tappity-tap-tap-tap! (That's me typing like a madman, hoping to beat my fellow passengers and secure a decent boarding number.) But when my boarding pass pops up… GROUP 7!

(Am I competing against professional typists?)

Group 7 is the equivalent of being picked last in PE.

Except the ticket agents are the captains, and not only do they NOT want me on their team, they don't think I deserve overhead bin space.

But I'm not always in Group 7. Sometimes I'm Group E.

"E" as in… EVERYBODY gets to board, but you!

This is why I decided it was time to try a new airline…

Delta.

When my boarding pass popped up last week, I almost fell out of my chair.

MAIN CABIN #2!

Are you kidding me?!

It was as if I were a silver medalist.

Delta likes me! They really like me!

I stood at my gate, beaming, boarding pass in hand, facing upward, in perfect scanning position.

"In just a few minutes, we will begin boarding," the agent announced in a cheery voice.

I extended my arm back and positioned my carry-on, so it was ready to roll. My right leg was forward, knee slightly bent. Obviously, I had already stretched.

"We will start with our Delta One passengers," the agent gushed, blowing them kisses.

That must be their fancy name for First Class.

That's okay, Main Cabin One will be next, and then, Moi!

After all the fancy pants people boarded, the agent announced, "Active Military, you may now board." She saluted them.

Not going to argue that one. Also, thank you for your service.

I edged forward. Any moment she'll be calling the good folks of Main Cabin #2.

"First Class and Delta Premium, you may now board." The agent gave them a round of applause.

I thought Delta One was First Class?! And what's this Delta Premium you speak of?

More fancy, smug people boarded.

But I didn't lose faith. I knew I was close.

"We now invite our Diamond Medallion members to board," the agent beamed.

I sighed.

As if I could compete with a club based on diamonds and medallions.

However, most of the Diamond Medallion members were wearing neither diamonds or medallions, so obviously it was a club based on lies.

"Families with small children, you may now board," the agent said, giving a thumbs up to the frazzled parents and their screaming toddler, who kept neither his hands nor his bronchial cough to himself."

But I had bigger problems. The herd had thinned, and overhead bin space was diminishing. I knew I had to get the ball rolling.

I raised my fist in the air. "Main Cabin! Main Cabin! Main Cabin!" I chanted, trying to engage my fellow cabin passengers. But they were a listless bunch, completely devoid of team spirit.

I slumped against a pillar as the agent welcomed, "Delta Comfort."

Still smiling, but with her enthusiasm waning, she announced, "Sky Priority, you may board."

A bunch of average Joes shuffled past me.

I'm losing to these guys?

"We will now board Main Cabin #1," she said, forcing a smile.

The below-average Joes boarded.

When there was only us riff-raff left, the agent yawned, "Main Cabin #2... I guess."

I dragged myself over to the agent. After scanning my boarding pass, she said, "We're out of overhead bin space, so you'll need to-"

"Yeah, yeah, yeah," I sighed, handing her my carry-on.

I guess that's what happens when you're in Main Cabin #2.

Which is the equivalent of Group 9.

> *"We now invite our Diamond Medallion members to board," the agent beamed.*
>
> *I sighed.*
>
> *As if I could compete with a club based on diamonds and medallions.*
>
> *However, most of the Diamond Medallion members were wearing neither diamonds or medallions, so obviously it was a club based on lies.*
>
> *"Families with small children, you may now board," the agent said, giving a thumbs up to the frazzled parents and their screaming toddler, who kept neither his hands nor his bronchial cough to himself."*

Also known as Group I.

And we all know what "I" stands for…

I can't believe I was excited about Main Cabin #2!

Down on My Puck

BOS TO LGA

Boston, Massachusetts, to
New York City, New York, September 1984
Written by
John Branning

One of the first business trips I took was to spend a week at my company's Boston office, filling in for a trainer who had taken ill as a new hire class had just gotten underway.

Class wrapped up early on Fridays, which meant I was able to book a late afternoon flight home. I flagged down a cab for the 15-minute ride to Logan Airport.

This was some years ago, long before the security protocols that have been in effect since 9/11 – back then, you could waltz into the airport and board a plane with nary a moment's hesitation. And I was counting on that, since my flight was scheduled to leave an hour after I got into that cab.

The fly in the ointment – Friday afternoon traffic, particularly in the crowded, pre-Big Dig, Boston downtown. The quick hop I was anticipating ended up taking over 45 minutes. I threw money at the cabbie before dashing into the terminal and searching for my gate. Once I spied the information display, I broke into a full sprint, reaching the gate *just* as it closed.

"That's my flight!" I hollered. The gate agent looked at me sternly, saying, "Sorry, pal – once the gate is closed, we can't reopen it." I'm sure I displayed a crestfallen expression. After a brief moment, the agent spoke to me again: "So, you're headed to New York, huh? You must be a Rangers fan." While I didn't follow hockey at all, I figured it was a way to get on this fella's good side, so I replied enthusiastically, "Yeah, LOVE the Rangers!"

He shot me another stern look, then exclaimed, "The Rangers SUCK! The Bruins kicked their asses!" But before I could mumble an apology for fake-rooting for the wrong team, he broke into a smile and opened the door to the jetway. "Have a good flight home."

I learned two lessons that day: 1) always plan enough time to get to the airport, and 2) display affection for the home team when you're on their turf.

That Was a Close One

ORD TO TPA

Chicago, Illinois, to Tampa, Florida
Shared by
Kevin Benjamin

It's pretty common to see security dogs at airports these days, all over the world. TSA uses them to sniff out anything from bombs to drugs, but their superb snouts weren't always utilized. In fact, it wasn't until 2008 that they became the norm. Screening technology, including body scanners, were being used a few years before that, after the 9/11 attacks in 2001. So, if you were flying before those dates, it would be no huge task to be able to hide some drugs somewhere on your body and likely get through airport security with no issues. And that was the case with Kevin on this particular day at Chicago O'Hare airport, as he was waiting to board a plane to head back to Florida.

My flight was running late, and I was passing the time reading a *USA Today* newspaper. I'd hidden a small bag of marijuana in my shoe before coming to the airport. No, it wasn't legal, but if nobody knew, what harm was there? Until I saw two FBI agents and two police officers walking straight towards me. My heart started racing. I buried my head in the paper, trying to peek without being obvious, using my peripheral vision. They were getting closer and closer, and I was starting to panic a little.

They were 10 feet away. I took a deep breath, just waiting to get busted.

Miraculously, they walked right past me, went into the terminal and walked out with New York City Mayor Rudy Giuliani, who had made the plane late because of his important arrival.

Now, THAT was close.

If they only knew.

Bison Balls and Lamb Penis

(We Promise This is Not X-rated)

LHR TO ORD

London, England, to Chicago, Illinois
Shared by
Páya from Prague

Many of us have four-legged, furry family members. And they can't always come with us on our travels. So, we arrange for their time away from us to be as painless as possible, and ask other loved ones to care for them in our absence.

That was the case for Páya from Prague, when she had to head to London for work. And in this case, SHE was the one who left those around her at the airport dumbfounded.

I was sitting at London Heathrow, on the phone with my boyfriend back in the U.S., who was taking care of our dog, Hurricane. The pup was on a raw diet, and I had pre-made meals for her ahead of time. But when I got delayed for a few days, my sweet pup ran out of her specialized food. So, I needed to walk my boyfriend through how to make more.

I'm sitting at the gate, giving him instructions.

"Take the big Ikea bag and put in it lamb penis, bison balls, sardines, some muscle meat, duck feet..."

I start noticing a couple odd looks in my direction.

My boyfriend tells me he has it, so I continue, telling him to let it thaw and then he could get into the prepping. So I keep going, "Ok baby, once it's all

"Ok baby, once it's all thawed you drain the fluids, you take two bison balls and chop them into small chunks. You add 50 grams of lamb penis. Don't forget that, that's her favorite! Half a sardine blended with freezer-dried pork brains, two chicken feet, add the muscle. Now, top it off with some blueberries and goat milk."

Then I said something like, "She's gonna love it. Tell my baby I love her. You guys enjoy your time together. Love you!"

I hang up with my boyfriend and THAT'S when I look around and see all their quite stunned faces.

thawed you drain the fluids, you take two bison balls and chop them into small chunks. You add 50 grams of lamb penis. Don't forget that, that's her favorite! Half a sardine blended with freezer-dried pork brains, two chicken feet, add the muscle. Now, top it off with some blueberries and goat milk."

Then I said something like, "She's gonna love it. Tell my baby I love her. You guys enjoy your time together. Love you!"

I hang up with my boyfriend and THAT'S when I look around and see all their quite stunned faces.

I process it all and realize they're hearing my special meal instructions, not knowing who I'm feeding lamb penis to, and they probably think I'm instructing him on some witchcraft ritual.

It was a very interesting moment.

And nope, no one asked for the recipe.

Passport Panic

BCN TO JFK

Barcelona, Spain, to
New York City, New York, October 2023

Anyone who's ever had to fly in or out of a country after losing their passport knows it's gonna be a headache without that all-important piece of ID. And more than that. It's gonna be time-consuming.

The Barcelona customs agent who rescued me before I knew I needed to be rescued.

My 18-year-old daughter and I were flying home from a dream trip to Europe on one of those crack of dawn morning flights that require you to get up at 4am. We were leaving Barcelona, Spain, and had to go through customs before walking to our gate. There was a short line, and when it was our turn, I was greeted by an attractive young woman who asked all the typical questions.

"Where are you going? Where have you been?"

I handed over our passports and made small talk, letting her know we were headed to JFK in New York after a really incredible trip that I hated to see end.

She sent us on our way with a smile, so we started walking toward our gate, where my exhausted daughter would likely go back to sleep while I kept watch for our departure.

I needed water and we were passing a vending machine, so I stopped to buy a bottle, while my daughter took our backpacks and headed to our gate to find a cozy seat to resume her sleep. As I was waiting for my water to come out of the machine, a woman rushed up to me, asking, "Are you Desiree?"

She was the same woman I had just met at the customs counter, and she was carrying the passport I had JUST shown her. The same one I *thought I put away in the front zipper pouch of my backpack.

She explained that the next person in line had come back and turned it in, saying they had found it on the floor as they exited customs. Immediately I thought, oh no, I had my passport AND my daughter's, so if mine fell out, hers probably did, too.

I explained that to the agent, who told me mine was the only one turned in, so we backtracked all the way to the customs desk, scanning the floor the entire way, hoping we would spot it on the ground or, by some miracle, someone else had turned it in while we were away.

Except, when we got back to the desk, her colleague was NOT happy with her. To me, she was a hero, tracking me down only going by my photo on my passport and the knowledge that I was flying to New York. But to him, she was a coworker slacking on the job of checking people through customs. The small line that was there when I went through customs was more like a mob in the short time she'd been away, and he didn't appreciate having to hold down the fort, so to speak.

She got the message that she needed to get back to work, but took my cell phone number, so she could call me if the missing passport turned up. I literally hugged her for finding me to return my passport, and thanked her for keeping on the lookout for the other one.

All the while, my daughter was comfortably resting back at the gate, oblivious to any issue until she saw me rush back, desperate to open my backpack. I figured there would be some slim chance that maybe her passport was still in that front pocket, despite the fact that mine had fallen out. I'm sure she had to wonder just how responsible her mother actually was, since she trusted me to hold her passport so she wouldn't lose it. The irony is not lost on me now, nor was it then.

So, I tore that pocket open, and there it was, like a hidden treasure. Her passport was still tucked away safe and sound.

And yes, after I caught my breath, I rushed back to the customs agent to let her know all was well in our world, thanks to her extra effort and a mini-miracle that I wasn't totally irresponsible that day. But I'm pretty sure my daughter is going to hold on to her passport herself from now on. Totally fair, kid. Totally fair.

When the Pilot Has Plans

JFK TO ATL

New York, New York, to Atlanta, Georgia
Shared by
Rob Andres

When there's bad weather, flying becomes especially challenging.

It's tough enough for airlines to make on-time departures when the weather is ideal, but when there's a hurricane out there, all bets are off. Usually.

But not if the pilot has somewhere to be.

Keep reading for our next tale from the terminal, from Rob in Atlanta.

I was working up in New Jersey on business. I had a flight home and was running late just getting to the airport. Hurricane Sandy was clobbering the coast and I had to maneuver my rental car through the storm and New York City streets when power was out, making the normally challenging drive even more daunting.

White-knuckled, I finally made it to the airport, where I dropped off the rental car and raced to security and on to the departure gate. I arrived just as they were closing the door to the jetway, as the attendant smiled and told me, "Just in time!"

Having done my part to make it on my flight, I hurried onto the plane and gathered my things at the front for a minute before squeezing my way down the aisle to my seat. I finally sat down, buckled up, and the guy beside me started making conversation.

"It's good you made the flight, but the next question is how long the plane has to sit here before being cleared for takeoff, if it happens at all, with the storm stirring up all these issues outside," he says.

I chuckle and tell him we are definitely going to make it on time.

"How could you possibly know that's true?" he asks.

But I had insider knowledge from when I was gathering my stuff just after stepping on the plane.

I tell him, "Well, I heard the pilot talking on his phone to one of his friends, apparently about going out tonight. I heard him say, very confidently, 'Don't worry, I'll be there ON TIME.' He's putting this plane in gear and getting us there, making up whatever time he has to in the air. No doubt!"

And, lo and behold, I was right. That flight DID arrive on time!

If only every flight had a pilot with a party to get to, right?

The Chain Reaction

DET TO ATL

Detroit, Michigan, to
Atlanta, Georgia, January 2017

After several days of being on my feet and "on my game" working as media at the Detroit Auto Show, in what I can only describe as running a marathon in heels, I was ready to get home. Worried about a winter storm that was starting to clobber us with wind and lots of snow, I got to the airport hours before I was supposed to, hoping to catch an earlier flight. Only problem was, everyone else was looking to do the same thing, so I sat. And I sat. And I sat some more. Not only did I NOT catch an earlier flight, but the weather was making it so incoming flights were delayed, and so were the outbound ones, including mine, that was supposed to leave at 7 pm.

If your flight was actually making it out, you were thrilled.

Unless you were these folks, sitting at the gate beside mine, where over the intercom, the airline staff announced, "We will be delaying boarding for the flight to Dallas. The flight coming in had a rough landing and a lot of people got sick, so they need to clean up the rows before we can let you board the plane."

Yes, that was a collective groan you just imagined, and that's exactly what I heard that evening, from the people who not only now were delayed, but also about to board a flight that was likely to smell, well, not good. I don't have to describe it. We all know that stench.

Let me tell you what…if that flight WAS going to my same destination, it would have been a hard NO if they'd offered me a seat.

I'm like most folks, who can handle my own vomit when I must, but have what I describe as "sympathy puking" when I hear another person start to get sick. Lord help us all if I have to smell it.

By the description in the announcement, "it was a rough landing and a lot of people got sick", I was imagining quite the mess. And just thinking about it had me starting to upchuck. Even writing this now, I can't help but feel a bit like barfing.

I, fortunately, didn't get on that flight, so I don't know for sure, but my gut tells me there was heaving, retching and gagging like a chain reaction. Not something I want to be buckled in for. Ever. Which made it much easier for me to sit and be patient for my flight, which ultimately did take off, finally, at 11 pm, vomit-free.

Feeling Lucky?

SJU TO ATL

San Juan, Puerto Rico, to Atlanta, Georgia
Shared by
Kip Renaud

Flying standby is a double-edged sword.

On one hand, any time you can fly somewhere for free, or close to it, is a great thing.

But on the flip side, there's never any guarantee you're going to make that flight.

You have to be a bit of a gambler, ok with knowing you'll win some and you'll lose some, so you just have to "go with the flow," as they say.

Well, not everyone is good with that, as we find out from the Renaud family.

We're used to flying standby, the four of us having done it for years, thanks to my job with Delta. On this particular flight, we were on standby to go from Puerto Rico to Atlanta, which is not a short flight, but not a trip to Europe, either.

We're used to sitting around and hoping, knowing we'll eventually get on a flight, if we're patient enough.

But the man sitting next to us at the gate that day was not. He was not good at it at all.

He was flying on what's called a "buddy" pass, which airline employees are given to share with friends or extended family, but it still means you fly only if there's space for you on the plane.

He realized we were flying standby and struck up a friendly, lengthy chat about the process. As an airline employee, I had access to inside information that let me know the odds of making one flight versus another, where we were in line to board, etc.

So this man persistently peeked over my shoulder, nervously asking, "How's it looking?"

He shared that, as an executive producer of reality shows, he needed to get back to the U.S. and HAD to make the next flight. We enjoyed his big city, high-energy conversation, but it was clear he was not at all comfortable playing the waiting game.

I occasionally checked my laptop, gauging how many other people were ahead of us on the standby list, how many seats might be available, essentially guessing the odds, while our fellow traveler asked for updates again and again and again.

Even our kids, 13 and 15 years old, explained to him there's not a lot you can do in this situation. You just have to wait it out.

In between pacing around the airport, making anxious calls on his cell phone and sweating, the producer kept asking, "HOW are you so relaxed? Aren't you worried about getting off this island? Even your kids are just playing on their phones! I'm going to write a new TV series called 'The CALM Renauds!' It'll be about people who don't get upset!"

He finally reached his breaking point, walked up to the gate agent and bought a ticket, paying the enormous last-minute fare to ensure he had a seat on the plane.

At boarding, he was the first in line to get on.

As luck would have it, our entire family also made it on the flight.

We boarded last, so we had to walk by our new friend who was sitting in his expensive seat. His eyes popped open when he saw us.

"You have GOT to be kidding me!" he exclaimed. "You ALL got on…and there was STILL room on the plane?"

We smiled, then settled into our seats.

Kind of reminds me of the famous quote, "The key to everything is patience. You get the chicken by hatching the egg, not by smashing it."

Time to Fly

EWR TO IAH

Newark, New Jersey, to Houston, Texas
Shared by
Jonathan B. Smith

Flight attendants have to deal with all kinds of craziness as part of their job, but this next unexpected incident is one for, well, the birds. Fortunately, they had a real wrangler on board, Jonathan B. Smith, who wasn't expecting that day to have to tap into skills he'd picked up in the past. He fills us in on the story of a sneaky stowaway from here.

I once got on a plane in Group 1, and as I entered the plane and looked down the aisle, I saw a pigeon.

The flight attendants were trying to catch it, but the bothersome bird kept evading their best attempts.

Well, my good friend had a cockatoo as a kid, so I was used to handling large birds. I had no desire to have to deboard the plane for them to get rid of it, or let the debacle lead to a delay on our flight, so I put my bag in the overhead and grabbed my Burberry overcoat (likely the world's most expensive bird net, but I digress).

I walked down the aisle and threw my coat over the pigeon. I then picked the coat up, holding the bird so that it couldn't escape, but also wouldn't be hurt.

The flight attendant asked me to pass her the pigeon, which I didn't consider a very wise move. In my mind, if she couldn't catch the bird, she wasn't going to be great at holding on to it, either.

So I looked at her like she was crazy and said let's walk back to the jet bridge.

We walked against the traffic of other people boarding, and got to the door by the jet bridge.

> "*I walked down the aisle and threw my coat over the pigeon. I then picked the coat up, holding the bird so that it couldn't escape, but also wouldn't be hurt.*
>
> *The flight attendant asked me to pass her the pigeon, which I didn't consider a very wise move. In my mind, if she couldn't catch the bird, she wasn't going to be great at holding on to it, either.*"

I prodded her to open it and she hesitated a bit, giving me a look that said she knew the TSA wouldn't approve. Well, it may have been a security violation, but at this point we both wanted the bird banned, so she opened the door. I opened my coat and the bird flew away.

For my troubles, I got a free drink and 2,000 airline miles, and a drycleaning bill for $25.

The way I see it, it was my good deed for the day and the flight departed on time!

Crisis averted!

CHAPTER FOUR
MAKING CONNECTIONS

One of my favorite parts about being at an airport is the knowledge that every day, thousands of people are brought together into one place, where their paths may intertwine for a matter of an hour or more, and then, by the end of the day, they'll all be separated again in different parts of the world. Sometimes, along the journey, they'll see familiar faces and make new connections, literally and figuratively.

The Lunch Layover

EWR TO PHX

Newark, New Jersey, to Phoenix, Arizona, late 1990s
Shared by
Michael Riordan

This trip starts in Newark Airport, in the late '90s, where Michael and two buddies are headed to Utah for a ski trip. Their connection is in Phoenix, where they have a three-hour layover.

We land at PHX and we're very hungry. We make it to the food court. I look over to my left and five feet away I see Walter Cronkite!

I can't believe I'm so close to the man who delivers the nightly news.

I tell my buddies, "Hey, that's Walter Cronkite!"

They say, "Bullshit....but if you think it's him, go ask him."

So I did.

"Excuse me, are you Walter Cronkite?" I say to the man considered the most trusted man in America at the time.

Mr. Cronkite politely responds, "Why, yes, I am. How are you? What is your name?"

Much to the shock of my pals, after a few back and forths, Mr. Cronkite invites me to sit down for a chat...for the next 45 minutes or so!

I had a really cool conversation with him. Just a wise, funny…maybe a touch lonely, or maybe just so nice and gracious to invite me into his world for that tiny piece of time. I'll never forget it.

It's hard to forget the people who treat you well on your travels, especially when they're the man you've seen in your home on the nightly news for decades.

Drop and Survive

DCA

Washington, D.C., 2000
By
William W. Hopper

This was in the summer of 2000, when you could go into an airport and get your ticket from a live agent who would check your bags. Then, you would walk right out onto the concourse, right to your gate.

It was the end of a fabulous weekend of parties and celebrations. My sister-in-law, Mary Ann, had just retired from a long career as a nurse, including 20 years in the Army, serving around the world, even during the Vietnam war. Friends came in from all over to celebrate with dinners and parties that stretched over a long weekend, ending in a quiet family dinner the night before she returned to her home in Indianapolis, Indiana.

I noticed a strange sight when I went into Washington National Airport (now Washington Reagan National Airport), a security guard. While today it is not an odd occurrence, back in the year 2000, it was not at all common. And I have to say. He was everything fantasies are made of. That hot policeman, a tall, striking stance with broad shoulders, square jaw, buzz cut, quite masculine looking. And as a gay man, I took notice.

We made our way to the ticket counter where a friend was working. He would often bump her up to First Class and did this day—a great way to end the weekend and send her home in style.

Mary Ann wanted to shop for souvenir trinkets for her mom's caregiver.

Washington National Airport had just been rehabbed with many shops, so we thought, let the search begin. We had gotten to the airport early, so we had all the time in the world. Starting at one end and walking up and down the various concourses shopping like in any mall. We both enjoyed and admired the architecture of the newly built terminal. Sadly, the various shops lacked what she was looking for - shot glasses with images of Washington D.C. on them.

As we strolled the concourses, I noticed the same hunky security guard a few more times. Not following us, but always on guard, nearby, and visible to me. While I did not mention it to Mary Ann, I thought it was odd for an airport to have one security guard who showed up everywhere.

As we entered the last shop, Mary Ann told me we must find them (meaning the shot glasses) as it was the very last shop. While she was browsing the souvenirs, I was looking at the magazines. I hear what sounds like someone dropping their luggage on the floor. I look around, and Mary Ann is nowhere to be seen. I step over to the souvenir display and see Mary Ann splayed out on the floor like a sack of potatoes. I yelled out to the shop clerk to call 911; Mary Ann has had a heart attack. I deduced this, as she had always had heart problems and had a heart valve replacement when she was in the Army in 1975, being the first member of the armed forces to stay in after such a significant surgery.

We called 911 – and they said, "Oh, you are at the airport. You will have to call for airport security."

Time was ticking, and we did that. Meanwhile, two people (one who turned out later to be a doctor, though he told me he was an Eagle Scout) stopped and provided CPR. Oddly enough, during that time, the same security guard appeared and spoke to me, telling me quite clearly that Mary Ann would be OK.

I looked at him and said, "Aren't you going to do something?" The airport police and EMS team arrived, took over from the "Eagle Scout" and proceeded to work on her. The Eagle Scout and his companion were very sincere, telling me that incidents like this were often not recoverable and that getting her to the hospital was the best thing. In the meantime, the security guard who spoke to me had disappeared, as did the Eagle Scout and his companion.

Mary Ann was loaded onto the stretcher and taken to an elevator, which was not designed to accommodate a stretcher. They had to tie her down tightly and stand her up as we descended to the tarmac. She was loaded into the ambulance and driven down a taxiway to an exit off the airport grounds – going through security, with several police cars escorting us to the hospital.

During this operation, I called her brother, my husband, and said we had an incident at the airport. Yes, there were basic cell phones at the turn of the 21st century. I did not want to tell him the whole story on the phone. I just asked that he come to the airport as soon as possible. While driving up the George Washington Parkway, he called and said he was passing a lot of police cars and an ambulance going the other way. “Where should I go?” he asked. I said turn around and follow those police cars and the ambulance that is us, and we are going to Arlington Hospital.

He arrived at the hospital just as she was being unloaded. I took his keys and parked the car, and during that time, the airport police were very solicitous to him, saying that they were very sorry that she had taken ill and not to expect a positive outcome. It turns out that heart attacks are more common at airports than one might expect. Upon my return, I asked them about the “security guard” I saw at the airport. And the airport policeman said to me, “We do not have anyone on our force who fits that description. Most of the force is here with me. Do you see him here?” I said no.

That night was a tough one as we called family and friends to let them know that Mary Ann had suffered a heart attack at the airport, and the prognosis was not good. Early the next morning, the phone rang. It was the ICU Nurse reporting that not only was Mary Ann up and conscious, but she was telling the nursing staff what to do. She had been a supervising nurse at a major hospital before her retirement.

They enjoyed that she was ordering them around and felt a camaraderie with her because of her career.

They also shared she had no recollection of what had happened and was confused about why she was in ICU.

A month later, after installing a pacemaker, she was cleared to go home to Indianapolis. We repeated the same process at the airport. She checked in, got the first-class bump, and we stopped at the shop where she had dropped. The same woman was behind the counter and recognized us. Telling us several people, including the "Eagle Scout," had been back to inquire about the woman who had fallen ill a month earlier.

Mary Ann got home to Indiana that afternoon, and the next day, a sweltering hot mid-western August Day, she decided that the landscapers had not mowed the lawn to her liking. So, she got out her own lawn mower to mow it properly. As she had done for years. At this point, the pacemaker kicked in several times. A neighbor took her to the hospital.

She told me later about a very handsome and hunky tall security guard who came up to tell her Mary Ann would be OK and then disappeared—describing the same man I had seen in Virginia a month earlier.

We all discussed this fellow's appearance and disappearance, and it was decided that he was Mary Ann's Guardian Angel. Most likely one of the soldiers she nursed while on the battlefields of Vietnam. Mary Ann named him Chris. Chris appeared one last time to her, not to us. Mary Ann said out loud, "Chris is here to take care of me," just before she passed away on Veterans Day 2007.

I Need More Cowbell

DUB

Dublin Airport, Ireland, 2014
(on a layover from a Baltimore to Boston
to Dublin to Rome flight)
Shared by Lara and Marc DiPaola

Before we get into this next airport adventure, I'm going to have to make sure you're familiar with what was considered one of the best Saturday Night Live sketches ever produced. It was written by cast member/comedian Will Ferrell and playwright Donnell Campbell and came out in 2000. It features the recording of the song, "Don't Fear the Reaper" by Blue Öyster Cult. Christopher Walken stars as a movie producer in the sketch, Ferrell as a cowbell player, who gets a bit carried away with his instrument, to the producer's delight, but much to the displeasure of his bandmates, which included Jimmy Fallon, Chris Parnell, and others. The sketch was so popular it became a pop culture catchphrase in America and even made it into the dictionary. It was big. And so was Will Ferrell.

Lara and Marc DiPaola were headed on an adventure overseas, leaving their home in Baltimore for a flight to Rome from Boston, with a 22 hour layover in Dublin. They both were experienced flyers, with Marc having served as a special agent for Homeland Security, and even doing a stint as a Federal Air Marshal for a bit. They dressed for comfort for the flight, Marc in his Will Ferrell t-shirt, with a graphic that read, "I need more cowbell!"

We'll let them take it from here.

The flight was easy enough, and when we landed in Ireland, we were eager to get off the plane and make the most of our quick layover in Dublin. We had less than a day, big plans, and were eager to make the most of it.

We deboarded, and made our way to immigration, following procedure.

We handed our passports to the agent, answered the required questions about who we were and what we were doing there. The agent handed us back our passports and we started to walk out but got stopped.

Yep, we all know, that's never for anything good.

The supervisor tells us we need to come with him.

He orders us to take a seat, and we know enough to do exactly as we're told.

I start wondering if we should show Marc's badge. He says no, let's see what they want first. But we're both stumped over why we need a secondary review by immigration agents.

Until the supervisor returns and tells us how much he loves Marc's shirt, and Will Ferrell, and asks if he could take a photo with us. Then other agents come over, asking to do the same. Our hope for a quick exit evolves into thirty full minutes of talk about Ferrell, cowbells, and comedy.

Eventually, we were released and sent on our way to see what we can of Dublin.

First stop, Temple Bar, and yes, we got stopped there four more times, by people who loved the t-shirt and weren't shy about saying so.

It turns out Ireland adores Will Ferrell, who proudly lets anyone who asks know that his ancestors came from County Longford. He even paid a special visit to the area with his father, after his dad researched his history and found all the Farrells (Ferrell is a variation of that) were from Longford. On his visit, when word got out that he was in town, hundreds of them showed up at the pub he was in and he "ended up drinking at some Irish lawyer's house at like two in the morning."

I don't think he was wearing the cowbell shirt then, though.

So Much More Than a Drink

DAL

Dallas Love Field, Texas, March 2016
By
Fadra Nally

There are really only two reasons to stop at an airport bar: to kill time or to have a drink. Or, most likely, both. In fact, both were my reasons when I made my way to a wine bar at Dallas Love Field last week.

When I'm heading home from a trip and I'm traveling by myself, I love to afford myself the time to sit and have a real meal before boarding my return flight. Usually, my schedule doesn't allow for such luxuries because I'm always running late. But sometimes it works out and you get more than that drink you were looking for.

As I glanced at the airport directory, I realized my options were limited. I could either head to some southwestern-ish burger bar, grab some fast food, or wait my turn for a first-come, first-serve spot at the wine bar. And I wanted some good wine.

After circulating through the small dining room, I found a few tables getting ready to empty but a man at the bar offered to give up his seats since he had a larger party. So, Heather and I sat down together at the bar.

Heather was simply the woman waiting in line for a seat and we just happened to sit down next to each other. But an hour or so later, I left with a huge smile on my face and felt lighter in spirit and NOT simply because of the excellent wine I consumed.

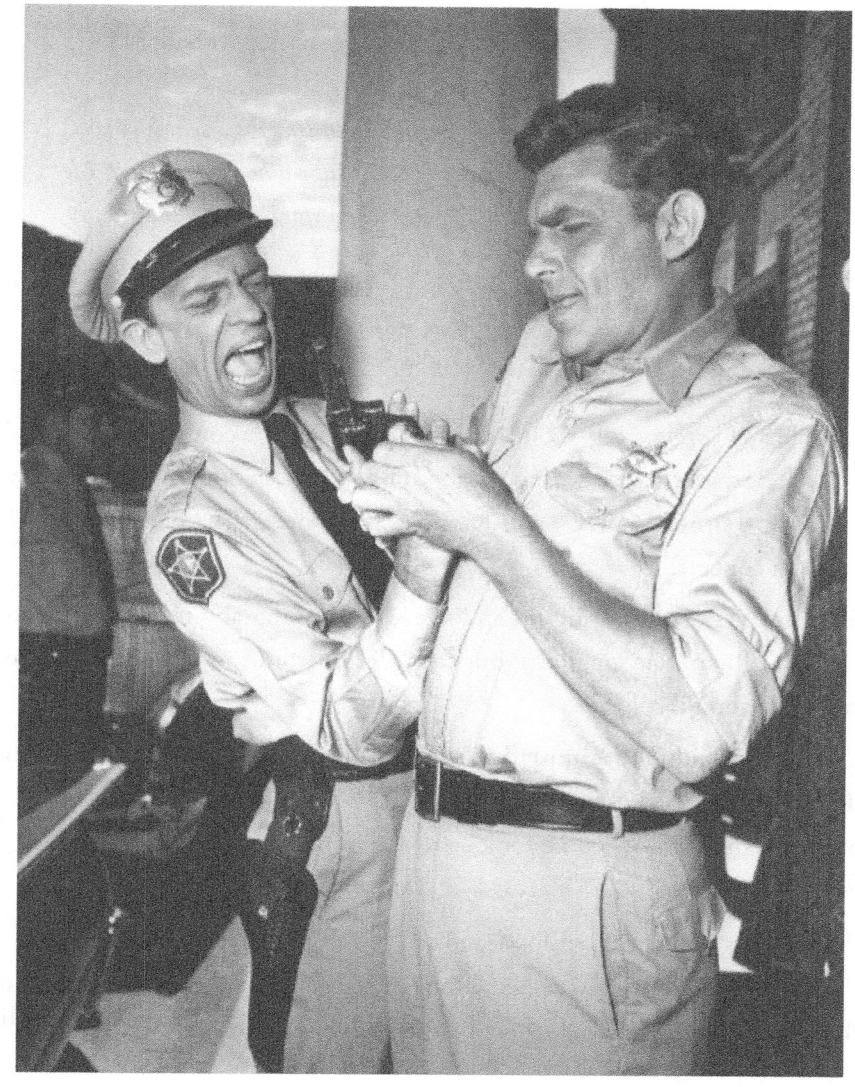

The bartender handed me a menu and gave off the "all business" vibe. He was there to take my order, hand me my check, and send me on my way. I ordered the "Old World" White Wines flight and Heather, contemplating which red to choose, thought my selection looked lovely and ordered the same.

> "*Heather was simply the woman waiting in line for a seat and we just happened to sit down next to each other. But an hour or so later, I left with a huge smile on my face and felt lighter in spirit and NOT simply because of the excellent wine I consumed.*"

We started by chatting about the wine and then the conversation turned to music. I made a joke to the bartender about the odd selection of music for a wine bar (Ozzy Osborne, AC/DC) and Heather asked me if I had ever been to Red Rocks for a concert.

Her birthday was coming up and she was thinking about buying tickets to see Gregg Allman. She giggled about the price of front row seats and wondered if maybe she should splurge.

Why not? I said. She admitted that she was a huge fan of Greg Allman and would love to be in the front row. *So go for it!* I suggested. Only recently, my husband did the same when he took us to the front row of the Imagine Dragons concert.

I asked if she liked good food and wine, and she did. I didn't even have to finish the thought before she realized the tickets were about the cost of two fancy lunches with her girlfriend. Tickets bought! I felt like her partner in crime, like we had conspired in some way.

We ordered more wine, shared my flatbread, and our conversation turned to television and movies. For reasons I can't remember, we started talking about our mutual fandom for *The Andy Griffith Show*, a show that my nine year old son has recently discovered on Netflix. Not only does he watch it, but he laughs in all the right places. It makes my heart swell with pride.

Talk of Andy Griffith turned to talk of Don Knotts and his comedic genius and that's where the bartender came back in. Mr. Business heard us talking about Don Knotts and asked if we had ever seen the movie, *The Ghost and Mr. Chicken*. Although I hadn't seen it, the bartender came to life recounting some of his favorite parts and we saw a small smile come across his face. Before we knew it, he had poured us a little extra and replaced my overcooked flatbread with a fresh one.

Heather gave me her card and I gave her a hug. She had lightened my spirit when I was just about ready to collapse. And it was my turn to do the same for someone else.

The soundtrack in the bar changed from heavy metal to 80s. I looked at the crowds sitting beside me and asked if they could name the band. The older crowd (looking roughly my age) looked at me as if I was crazy. But I insisted they try to recapture some of their youth.

When I was met with blank stares (although the bartender knew the right answer), I heard someone behind me whistling along with the song. I turned around quickly and said, "Name the band!" Which he did and we had a laugh. (The song, by the way, was "And We Danced" by The Hooters).

I pushed again when the next song came on. *Surely you know who sings this one, right?* Again, I had blank stares. I'm not sure if they thought I was crazy or if they just wanted to be left alone but I turned to my musical cohort behind me and said *Name the singer!* Sure enough, he got Kenny Loggins.

And then, one of the men next to me slowly turned and said, *I know what movie it's from!*

It was from *Caddyshack,* so of course he knew the song.

My time was up and my flight was getting ready to board. Off I went waving farewell to the people I'd never see again. I remembered the smile Heather put on my face, the smile we put on the bartender's face, and thought about the smiles that might come to the others as I left the bar.

Every day, every encounter is a story waiting to happen. We just need to draw out the characters sometimes.

The Key to Comedy

ATL

Atlanta, Georgia, late 1980s
Shared by
Michael Riordan

Years ago, you could walk your family and friends to their gate at the airport when they were leaving. You didn't need a ticket or anything. It was before security was stepped up, and pretty common to just hang out with them until they boarded their plane and took off.

This is what 20-year-old Michael was doing with a buddy at the Atlanta airport, when his cousins were departing to head back to their home up north. He hugged them all goodbye and went to leave the airport, but realized he'd lost his car keys. What happened next was good and bad all at once.

We launched a feverish search, with us asking anybody and everybody if they'd seen these missing keys. It was getting late and unlike now, where the airport seems to be open all night, things were pretty much shutting down. We were in a desperate situation, with no real ride and running out of time to find a solution.

Out of nowhere, I see this guy who looks a lot like Jay Leno walking towards us. He was all alone, with literally no one behind him…like he was the next to last person in the airport. So, I walked up to him and asked "Jay Leno?"

It was like a weird dream, but real.

We proceed to tell him that we have been looking for the keys for over two hours, have no ride and yada, yada, yada. He offers us a ride home in his limo!

> *Out of nowhere, I see this guy who looks a lot like Jay Leno walking towards us. He was all alone, with literally no one behind him...like he was the next to last person in the airport. So, I walked up to him and asked "Jay Leno?"*
>
> *It was like a weird dream, but real.*
>
> *We proceed to tell him that we have been looking for the keys for over two hours, have no ride and yada, yada, yada. He offers us a ride home in his limo!*
>
> *Of course, we agree, and we take about five steps with him until we hear, over the intercom, "Would the gentlemen who lost his keys please report to gate whatever?"*

Of course, we agree, and we take about five steps with him until we hear, over the intercom, "Would the gentlemen who lost his keys please report to gate whatever?"

We were not devastated, but really didn't want to hear that 'good news'.

So, Jay was gracious and cracked a few jokes and was on his way...without us.

So close, yet so far, right Michael?

Who's the Nature Boy?

Charlotte, North Carolina
Shared by
Daniela Davenport

As you just read in our last essay, you could go all the way to the gate to say goodbye to family and friends back in the '90s, but you could also be waiting there when your loved one came off a plane. And that was the case for Daniela's husband in the Charlotte airport on this particular trip in 1995.

Standing there waiting for his ginger bride to come off the galleyway into the terminal, it was a blonde who took his breath away. A tall, very toned blonde at that. But in this case, it was no woman who had him speechless. It was the pro wrestler Ric Flair, AKA "The Nature Boy". As most boys who grew up watching the great wrestlers of those days, he was stunned to see this icon walking off the flight.

Then he saw his wife, Daniela.

My husband met me with an, "Oh my God, you were on the plane with Ric Flair!"

I didn't have a clue in the world who he was or what he looked like. A lot of people were coming up to him excited to get his autograph and crowding around him. So that's when I realized I'd been sitting right next to him in first class, but completely unaware that I should've known who he was.

During the flight, people kept walking by him and asking him to "Say that thing you say,"

He'd reply with odd things, like "Wooo!" and "To be the man, you've gotta' beat the man."

That probably should have been a tip-off that something was noteworthy about him, but honestly, even if he'd introduced himself, I wouldn't have known who he was.

And that's the beauty of airports and airplanes. They bring all kinds of people "in the ring" together. Famous and infamous, or just the average Joe, just trying to get to the next destination, but hopefully not fighting their way there.

I'm Proud of You, Kid

ORD

Chicago, Illinois
By
Susan LaMotte

I choked up when I got off the plane at O'Hare on Friday. Grief can hit you at any moment.

I don't fly through Chicago often and I found myself at the exact spot where I once randomly ran into my Dad in the airport. We were both on business travel (before cell phones) and I knew he'd be in Chicago, but our meeting was unplanned and unexpected.

We hugged. He laughed at my stiletto heels (why would you wear those through an airport, he wondered?). I was maybe 24 and an HR consultant. He was an exec with a top engineering firm. He worked his whole life for that job.

I don't even remember what city I was headed to, but I had won those high heels in a company contest (they used to have random contests where if you were the first to renew business with a client in that hour you'd win a gift card--and I won one from Nine West Group).

I was off to a big meeting, and he had such a big smile on his face and congratulated me on working so hard. He told me how proud he was of me.

My dad is now eight years into an Alzheimer's diagnosis. He's long retired, but loved his corporate jobs. He doesn't know my name anymore and can't say much. But he already said what he needed to.

It made me realize how important it is for us to tell our kids we're proud of them. No matter what job they have, including being a stay-at-home parent. Tell them you see them. No matter how old they are. It will stick with them forever.

What Happened in Vegas...

LAS

Las Vegas Airport, Nevada, 1981
By
Karen Bucci

My husband Jack and I were married in early 1980. Six months later I was pregnant with our first child. Shortly after that, in late 1980, Jack was given a promotion at work and transferred from Ohio to San Jose, California. We had our first child, a daughter, in California in April 1981.

We were in our early 20s, still newlyweds, first time parents, and basically alone. Life in California was very different and expensive, from the weather, to the food, to long-distance phone calls, and especially the cost of living. We could barely afford the high rent we paid for our small condo, and could only call our family once each per month.

We terribly missed our families and wanted to share our new baby girl with everyone. Jack worked for an overnight air freight company, and they had an agreement that you could fly standby on a certain passenger airline for a very, very reduced price.

It was the only way we could afford to fly home, and we were so grateful. When our daughter was about 10 weeks old, we flew standby from California to Cleveland, Ohio.

We made it to Vegas, but got bumped there and ended up having to spend the night in the Las Vegas airport. With a newborn baby. In theory, we understood that we could get bumped off a flight we booked, but we assumed we would wait an hour or two and get on the next flight. Well, the next flight wasn't until the next day.

Airports were very different 40 plus years ago. All of the agents, flight attendants, pilots, and airport police were very polite and helpful. One of the police officers saw us wandering around with the baby and struck up a conversation. We told him what had happened and that we would be there for the night. He was very friendly and sympathetic. We saw him several times during the course of that night and he would stop to see how we were.

At some point in the evening, we found a waiting area that kind of resembled a living room with comfortable chairs and side tables. We made a fort of sorts and formed a circle with chairs and tables, with the baby's car seat in the middle of the circle on the floor. We took turns dozing and keeping watch over her. I was breastfeeding so there was no shortage of food, and we had plenty of diapers and clothes in our carry-on bags. She was not used to the change in her routine, so part of the night was spent walking with her up and down the airport trying to get her to fall asleep. Neither of us had ever been to Vegas, and we were amazed to see slot machines in the airport. I got so used to wandering around with her over my shoulder that I grabbed a few quarters from my wallet and walked over to put them in a machine. It was all I could afford, and I was sure I would be done in a minute or two. A man swiftly approached and gently told me that no one under 18 was allowed to be on the gaming floor. It took me a minute to realize he meant my baby girl. She was definitely under 18! I guess I was starting her gambling habit young.

Late in the evening, when the last flights were done and things got quiet, a man came to the area we had commandeered and sat down in a chair about 20 feet away. He was dressed nicely, with black hair and darker olive skin. He looked like he was from another country, maybe Greece or Lebanon. We exchanged glances but did not speak.

He didn't bother us and we didn't bother him.

Sometime in the middle of the night Jack noticed that the man had walked away and left his wallet and watch on the arm of the chair he had been sitting on. He mentioned it to me, and I told him that we should keep an eye on it until he returned. It never even occurred to us to touch the wallet or look inside. A couple of hours later the police officer came over to us and asked us if we knew the man that had been sitting there. We told him we had not ever spoken to him, but he had left his watch and wallet.

He went over and picked them up and walked away with them.

Sometime later he came back and told us that the man had approached him and another officer that were standing together near the boarding area, got down on his knees, started bowing and praying to Allah, and told them he had a bomb! He was quickly subdued, and after he was searched, they realized he did not have a bomb. The officer then told us that there was $10,000 in cash in his wallet! After he walked away we sat there in shock for a few minutes. Finally, Jack looked over and said to me "We could have taken the money from his wallet, and flown first class to Hawaii. No one would have ever believed him if he told them he had that much cash in his wallet." His sarcastic macabre sense of humor was just what we needed. We both had a good laugh and it helped break the tension.

In a strange twist of fate, 20 years later I was working on my birthday trying to finish everything before we left the next day to meet our friends for a vacation in Vegas when the planes hit the twin towers. It was 9/11/2001. Needless to say, our flight was canceled, and we didn't go. Vegas, baby.

Parting the Red Sea

IAD TO CDG

Washington, D.C., Dulles Airport to
Paris, France, Charles de Gaulle Airport, April 2015
Shared by Keryn Means

It was going to be a dream trip. Keryn Means and her hubby, Mike, were off to Paris, to soak in the sights; the Louvre, the Eiffel Tower, and to eat all the French pastries and more. They were bringing their kiddos, five-year-old Deklen and toddler Tiernan, who was going to turn three on the trip. It was definitely going to be an adventure. But there was another adventure set to happen first.

We were all checked in and through security, had made it to our gate, and almost instantly connected with another family with young children who were there. We were sitting on the floor, letting the kids run around to get out all the energy they could before boarding a plane where we'd have to sit for hours.

My husband let me know he was off to fill our water bottles. We discussed whether he should take the little one but decided against it. After all, the kids were having a grand time.

So, Mike goes off to get the water and I keep chatting with the other parents we'd met, the kids all playing around us.

A couple minutes later, a woman walks up to our group playing on the floor and asks, "Are any of you missing a child?"

"No," we all reply, confident our kiddos are right there with us.

Only they aren't.

As I look around to confirm my two are all good, I realize Tiernan, my almost three-year-old, is gone!

An immediate terror takes over.

We're fortunately at the very end of a terminal, so I know he could have only gone in one direction.

I bolt up, tell the five-year-old to stay put with the other family, and go sprinting down the hallway, screaming his name.

The panic is clear in my voice and the crowds part like the Red Sea, giving me a clear path to search for my little one.

I'm delirious and it shows. And they're kind enough to get out of my way.

"Tiernan," I shriek, over and over, looking frantically left to right for my little guy.

I spot my husband at the water fountain, yell to him that our son is missing!!

Mike is confused. He's wondering what I'm yelling about. It couldn't be that our son, who he had just seen minutes before, has vanished. And as he's processing this, a miracle happens.

We both see him, a few steps away, not far at all from the water fountain.

Mike scoops up little Tiernan and holds him tight.

I'm out of breath, both from running and from relief.

My heart is beating out of my chest because I just went from the worst thing possible happening to the best thing possible, all in the span of a minute, a minute where all time stood still while total dread raced through my mind.

Once I caught my breath, I asked him why he wandered off. My little guy said he heard his daddy was getting to water, so he decided to follow him. Makes perfect sense in the mind of a toddler.

> *A couple minutes later, a woman walks up to our group playing on the floor and asks, "Are any of you missing a child?"*
>
> *"No," we all reply, confident our kiddos are right there with us.*
>
> *Only they aren't.*
>
> *As I look around to confirm my two are all good, I realize Tiernan, my almost three-year-old, is gone!*
>
> *An immediate terror takes over.*

I definitely strapped him into his stroller a little tighter on that trip, and for a while after. I know there are three or four times in parenthood that shake you to your core, and this was one for the books. And, thank goodness, it had a happy ending.

Years later, we're able to laugh about it all, "Hey, remember that time we lost you in the airport?", we joke, thankful that it didn't have a very different outcome.

Just Being Human

ATL

Atlanta, Georgia Airport, January 2024
Shared by
Cindy Tutko

Anyone who's walked through Atlanta's Hartsfield-Jackson Airport knows it's massive. It's been named the world's busiest airport for many years, and it's multiple concourses (T, A, B, C, D, E, and F) are connected by what they call the "Plane Train", a subway of sorts that transports about 286-thousand passengers each and every day.

There are 2,100 flight arrivals and departures daily, and on this day in early 2024, Cindy Tutko was one of them.

I had been visiting my son and his family in Louisiana and had a layover in Atlanta, on my way home to Florida. My incoming flight landed at Concourse C, and my next flight was taking off from Concourse F. Not a huge deal on most days, thanks to the Plane Train. But on this particular day, the train wasn't running. And I was dealing with a bad leg. I had a torn ACL and needed knee surgery, something that was scheduled in a month, but certainly not helpful on this particular day.

Without the Plane Train, I had to suck it up and walk. And walk some more. And then even more. All while I was carrying a full, heavy satchel and rolling a carry-on suitcase behind me. I was hurting. And people were passing by me, unaware of or indifferent to the pain I was in, just trying to make it to my next flight.

But Michael Wright didn't just pass me when he saw me limping along. He offered to help. Skeptical that he may just run off with my stuff, I told him no thanks, knowing I couldn't run after him if he bolted. But he offered again, and didn't wait for me to say no. He took my satchel and threw it over his own arm, then walked beside me.

I knew at that point that he was just being kind.

And he kept being kind, talking with me and walking for the near hour it took to get from Concourse C, past D, past E, and ultimately to my gate at F. And as we approached her gate, he grabbed my hand and said, "You're my mom". I was confused, until he started telling the gate agent that I was his mother, and had issues with my knee, so he wanted to know if I might be able to board early because it would take me a bit longer to get to my seat. The gate agent told him no problem, and we said our goodbyes.

I told Michael, "Your mom would be proud of you," then gave him a hug and small kiss on the cheek. I didn't get his number, but in our walk had found out his name was Michael, and he was from Lafayette, Louisiana.

So, when I told my son about this nice man and his kindness, my son put a post on social media to try to find him and thank him, too. Incredibly, it only took about a day.

> "*But Michael Wright didn't just pass me when he saw me limping along. He offered to help. Skeptical that he may just run off with my stuff, I told him no thanks, knowing I couldn't run after him if he bolted. But he offered again, and didn't wait for me to say no. He took my satchel and threw it over his own arm, then walked beside me.*
>
> *I knew at that point that he was just being kind.*
>
> *And he kept being kind, talking with me and walking for the nearly hour it took to get from Terminal C, past D, past E, and ultimately to my gate at F.*"

Michael's gesture got him recognition beyond me and my son, though. Local TV stations chose to highlight this act of kindness, too, which humbled Michael, who said he didn't do anything. He said he was "just being a human being."

But that's the thing these days. Not everyone is willing to get involved. To help when needed. To be human. Michael saw it as nothing, but it was everything to me that day, and to my son who couldn't be there to help. Turns out being human is all any of us need to be to make a difference in someone else's life.

Bumped and Benefited

IND TO DCA

Indianapolis, Indiana,
to Washington, D.C.
By
William W. Hopper

We would visit Indianapolis, Indiana, for Mother's Day to see my mother-in-law. It turns out that mid-May is also qualifying race weekend for the Indy 500. Many people descend on "Naptown" during that time to see the races.

While we were not doing anything race-related, our visit went according to plan. Well, until we got to the airport on Sunday afternoon and headed to the terminal to catch our flight from Indy to DCA. Being self-employed, I had not scheduled the day after as a workday, though my husband had to get to the office as planned. We never thought twice about the race, though it was unusually busy for a Sunday afternoon when we got to the airport. We both forgot that everyone would be heading home at the same time.

During check-in, we were asked if we would give up our seats for a later flight to our destination and a ticket for anywhere the airline flew in the USA later in the year. It was an easy decision for me to say yes. Dave boarded the flight back to DCA, and I was given the flight credit and booked on the next flight, the day's last flight. They asked if I would like to wait in the executive lounge until that flight took off. I gladly agreed to that.

The rescheduled flight also turned out to be overbooked. And I was again saying, why not? This time, I could choose my flight home and was again given another flight credit, as well as a hotel stay and a dinner voucher. Since we had just packed one bag, which flew home with David, I was happy to accept a toiletries kit. I did not book the first flight out in the morning, thinking I might want to sleep in, so I booked a 10 am flight home the following day. I used my dinner voucher at one of the restaurants at the airport, grabbed the hotel shuttle, and snuggled in for the night.

Getting to the airport on the shuttle the following morning was just as easy as getting to the hotel the night before. Without baggage, I went right up to the gate. And the story repeated itself when I was asked if I would give up my seat on this flight, Since I was already holding two tickets, I said, why not for a third?

I was bumped again, and then again on both the 1 o'clock and the 3 o'clock flights. However, I have to say, by mid-afternoon, I was ready to give up on this nonsense. The five flight certificates were enticing and not a bad haul for sitting around in the executive lounge.

In the end, I only used three of the tickets myself and could use the other two to give a friend for her birthday to fly to Denver to see her daughter.

As they say, time is money, and I made more in flight credits in the 24 hours than I would have made back home. Since that time, I have never been able to cash in quite like that Mother's Day Flight. Though I always think, will I do it again?

Best Thanksgiving Meal Ever

LGA TO ATL

New York City, New York, to
Atlanta, Georgia, November 24, 2016

After a double knee surgery that she nearly didn't survive (literally, they struggled bringing her back out of the anesthesia sleep-like state they'd put her in for surgery), I decided it was time to make one of my mom's bucket list wishes happen. She was a massive fan of the Macy's Thanksgiving Day Parade, putting it on the television to watch broadcast live pretty much every Thanksgiving

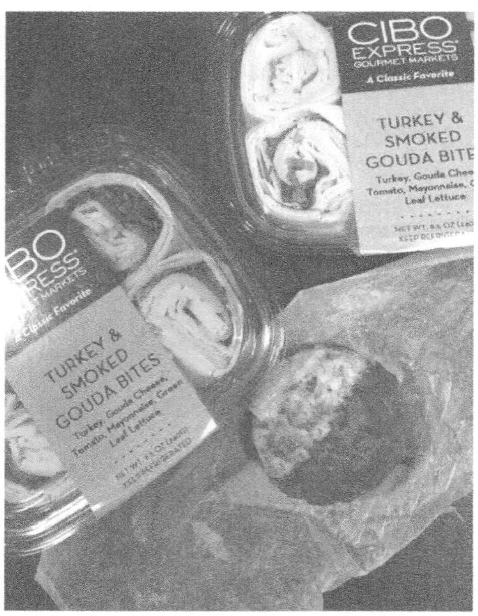

Our delicious Thanksgiving airport meal

morning of my childhood, and it became a tradition I continued throughout my life, knowing it was something she was likely watching, too, at her home 500 miles aways from me. So, when she had her big scare, I booked a trip for her to go see the parade in person, knowing it would be a massive hassle, since she couldn't get around well having not fully recuperated from her surgery, but thinking I didn't want to waste another year not making this bucket list trip happen.

> *We knew we weren't going to make it home in time for a big holiday meal, so we decided we'd just grab our dinner at the airport. Being in NYC, I was fully prepared to have to settle for a slice of pizza and be perfectly content after the memorable morning we'd had with the parade, but the airport surprised us.*
>
> *We were able to find a little ready-made sandwich shop offering up wraps, turkey and smoked gouda to be exact. And the bakery next door had my favorite chocolate-covered coconut macaroons, too. This simple meal could not have been more delicious if we'd been sitting at the very best restaurant in all of NYC.*
>
> *Our bellies were full, and so were our hearts, and to this day, it's one of my favorite Thanksgiving meals ever.*

When I shared more about planning the trip with friends on social media, they helped make it extra special, even contacting friends who worked backstage for the Rockettes Christmas Spectacular and setting it up so we could go backstage after the show and see how they made the magic happen. We wheeled her all around the Big Apple, seeing the floats inflate the night before the parade, watching Wicked on Broadway, going to the 9/11 Museum, taking the bus tour around the city to see all the famous sites. I even booked a hotel directly on the parade route to make it easy to come and go if she needed to go to the bathroom or anything that morning for the several-hour event. It was a whirlwind few days making memories, and when the big morning arrived to watch the parade, we got up at 4am, walked outside and grabbed front row seats on the curb, with enough room for her wheelchair to also have a view that wouldn't be blocked. It was freezing cold, but we bundled up and enjoyed every minute of it!

We had a flight back home that same day and I worried a bit about actually flying on the holiday, but I have to say, it was the best decision I could have ever made.

The airport has a calm feel to it when it's not overrun with people rushing here and there, and that's exactly what it's like on the actual Thanksgiving holiday. The days around this holiday are some of the busiest all year, but the Thursday when the rest of the world is sitting around their family's tables is pretty peaceful in the airport.

We knew we weren't going to make it home in time for a big holiday meal, so we decided we'd just grab our dinner at the airport. Being in NYC, I was fully prepared to have to settle for a slice of pizza and be perfectly content after the memorable morning we'd had with the parade, but the airport surprised us.

We were able to find a little ready-made sandwich shop offering up wraps, turkey and smoked gouda to be exact. And the bakery next door had my favorite chocolate-covered coconut macaroons, too. This simple meal could not have been more delicious if we'd been sitting at the very best restaurant in all of NYC.

Our bellies were full, and so were our hearts, and to this day, it's one of my favorite Thanksgiving meals ever.

My mom, who now struggles with Alzheimer's, doesn't remember the meal at all, but she does remember the rest of the trip, and that fills my heart more than any meal could fill my belly.

The Kindness of Strangers

VFA TO JNB

Victoria Falls, Zimbabwe, to
Johannesburg, South Africa, 2008
Written by
Eric Webber

Holidays can be challenging when you're traveling, and may be especially difficult if the place you're traveling to is going through a financial crisis. But it can leave you with priceless lessons, as Eric Webber and his family found.

In 2008, my wife and two sons (9 and 13 at the time) took a trip to several countries in southern Africa. On our way out of Botswana back to South Africa, we made a stop in Victoria Falls at the Zimbabwe border. We toured the falls and then were scheduled to take a flight to Johannesburg. The airline had a daily 737 flight from Johannesburg to Victoria Falls to Livingstone, Zambia, and back to Johannesburg.

The day we got to Victoria Falls, Christmas Eve, the economy of Zimbabwe was in a freefall. The Zimbabwe dollar had fallen from 500,000 = 1 USD, to 2,000,000 = $ 1 USD, in only a few days. The country was on the verge of abandoning its currency, but everything seemed to be OK otherwise. The locals seemed to take it in stride, and there was concern, but definitely no panic.

We got to the airport and were all hungry, so we went to the only restaurant there. When we arrived, an older gentleman was finishing writing up the specials on a chalkboard. "Best T-Bone Steak in Zimbabwe" was at the top of the list.

We were the only customers and ordered Cokes and a couple of beers from the young waitress. We chatted her up a bit and she was especially engaging with my sons. When she came back with our drinks, we ordered food; chicken and hamburgers as I recall. But she came back shortly after to tell us they were out of those items, so we all re-ordered. Another round trip from the waitress brought the same response. Next the manager came out, the same man writing on the sign earlier. He sheepishly told us they were completely out of food. I think it must have been difficult for him to admit that, as he seemed very proud of his restaurant.

We ordered another round of drinks, which were ridiculously cheap, and left a decent (but nothing crazy) tip on top of the bill. The waitress caught us just out the door to tell us we'd overpaid. When my wife told her that we hadn't, she couldn't have been more grateful.

We headed to our gate, stopping to buy some of the few snacks they had at the airport gift shop.

It was just about the time we should have been boarding but we noticed there was no plane there. At first, the airline representative said the flight hadn't yet left Johannesburg because of bad weather, a dubious claim since it was clear outside.

We found a quiet place to wait and watched the airline staff grow more worried, and the waiting passengers more restless.

Seemingly out of nowhere, the restaurant manager appeared with a large plate of French fries for my sons, who were starving by now. He apologized that it was the only thing he could find in his restaurant, and he thanked us for being so kind to his daughter, the waitress. He adamantly refused to take a dime for what turned out to be, under the circumstances, a great meal. He also told us that he'd talked to the local manager of our airline and learned that the plane wasn't coming at all. The airline was refusing to land in Victoria Falls. It was going to be charged the usual landing fee using the official government rate, which was now only a fraction of the actual exchange rate. So, they decided to just skip the stop instead.

By now, the local airline rep was more forthcoming, at least telling the passengers who had gathered at the gate that the flight wouldn't be arriving that day. They offered to put everyone up at a hotel and get us all out the next day, assuring us that the schedule would be worked out. He didn't mention the landing fee. My wife looked at me and said, "There's no way they're going to work this out on Christmas Day."

Quite a few of the passengers seemed willing to accept the offer. But a handful of us cornered the airline rep and negotiated another deal; we understood the flight was now going straight from Johannesburg to Livingstone. So, the airline agreed to hold it there for an additional hour to allow any of us who wanted to take the chance to drive the hour or so from Victoria Falls to Livingstone to catch it. Enough people agreed that the airline then offered to find a bus to take us.

And once again, the restaurant manager came to our aid. He was concerned the airline wouldn't find a bus in time, so he'd called his brother-in-law, a local tourist driver, to take us to the Zambian border. We grabbed an Australian couple we'd befriended and headed out. The van was already idling out front.

We got dropped off at the Zambian border. It cost us $20 U.S. for the drive for all six of us, plus we left extra for the driver and the restaurant manager and his family.

Now we had to get tourist visas, which were normally $100 per person. I use the term "normally" loosely, because the rate seemed to be determined by the circumstances. I negotiated it down to $100 for the family, plus the Timex Ironman digital watch I was wearing, since the customs agent admired it.

Our Zimbabwean driver had called ahead and arranged a driver from the Zambian frontier to the Livingstone airport. Another twenty bucks and we made it to our waiting flight.

We couldn't have been happier. The Livingston – Johannesburg passengers, who'd been made to wait 90 minutes on the plane for the 30 or so people who made the trek from Vic Falls, weren't nearly as thrilled.

We finally got to Johannesburg just before midnight. The airline put us all up in a gaudy casino hotel, where we woke up and celebrated Christmas the next day.

Not a typical Christmas morning in any way, but one of our most memorable, special because it was a wild ride, but more because of the lessons we all learned from the kindness of complete strangers.

It's Who You Travel With… or Who You Don't

Shared by
Carrie from Prineville, Oregon

It can be stressful for people to fly. It can be more stressful when they're flying with family members who they tend to argue with. That's evident any given day at any given airport, if you watch long enough.

My boyfriend and I were people-watching at the Seattle airport, waiting for a connecting flight, when we saw a woman in what looked like her late 50s, and daughter in her 30s, along with a granddaughter. They had all of their suitcases stacked up on a luggage cart and were arguing about something, being really hateful with each other.

I elbow my boyfriend and say, "What do you think they're arguing about?"

We were eavesdropping but couldn't really figure the argument out.

But then, the older woman walks down the terminal with her granddaughter, looking like they're going to find a restroom. The daughter starts rearranging all the luggage on the cart.

I ask my boyfriend, "What do you think she's doing?"

We're both stumped as we watch her take all the luggage off, then put it back on.

That's when my boyfriend tells me, "She's going to leave her mom's luggage on the ground!"

I tell him there's no way. Nobody would do that, right?

Well, she did.

The woman turned around and pretended like she didn't see the bag sitting there, and then just headed down the terminal with the rest of the bags.

I started to worry that with an unaccompanied bag, security would have to evacuate the terminal, because that happened to me once before at the Portland airport. I knew it wasn't a security risk, so I sat with my boyfriend and watched as people tripped over the bag, stared at the bag, but nobody reported it. Then, eventually, I spotted the older woman running down the terminal, cussing the entire way. She grabbed her bag and took off again.

It's definitely one of the strangest things I've ever seen happen at an airport, and we can only imagine how the rest of that trip went for that trio.

AirTroductions

DFW TO IAH

Dallas, Texas, to Houston, Texas, 2006
Shared by
Peter Shankman

Just like a good boss can make or break your life at work, a good seatmate can make or break your life in the sky. But Peter Shankman aimed to change that with his post-flight epiphany.

I sit down for my hour-long flight to Houston and beside me is a real beauty. Like really. She is Miss Texas. Literally.

So, as a friendly, single guy in my 20s, I strike up a conversation.

It turns out she's nice, too.

Our time in the air flies by and it's over all too soon.

Over the next few weeks, I take a few more flights.

But I don't have nearly as much fun.

And it hits me!

Wouldn't it be nice to sit next to someone you'd LIKE to sit next to on each and every flight?

Why CAN'T we do that?

So, I invent a company that makes it possible.

It's called AirTroductions, and gives a different meaning to "making your flight connections."

At first it wasn't really about dating.

It was just designed to link people with similar interests.

The idea was, you'd buy your ticket, then enter that info into our database, and if someone else had the same itinerary, you could be notified and arrange to have your seats together.

It was interesting. And fun. And some people really bonded.

But it didn't really grow much, until…well, until we heard from Lisa Loeb. Famous for her songs like "You Say" and "Fools Like Me", the celebrity was starting a reality show. Her producers reached out asking if they could use our services to set her up on an in-flight date. And what they produced ended up being the show pilot.

Well, that helped AirTroductions take off, literally. And it evolved into a dating site on the spot.

It was a fun few years, and I eventually sold the company to a private equity firm. Sadly, like so many other old flight options, it's no longer in service.

There IS one dating site set up for the airline industry, but it's only between pilots and cabin crew. However, every couple of years, an airline will announce it's starting a dating service for passengers in the air, but that's typically just an April Fool's joke. I think they should keep trying. I know of more than one couple who fell in love mid-flight (see our story called My Eternal Seatmate).

Friday Night Fun

ATL TO DHN

Atlanta, Georgia, to Dothan, Alabama, 2015
Shared by a friend who preferred not to share her name

When I was in high school, I was in love with this guy. We'll call him Rob. He was so popular and good looking, and I was as in love as a 15-year-old girl could be. But he never really saw me as anything more than friends, and we never dated, much to my massive disappointment.

Years later, he ended up dating a gal who was in one of my classes in college. I'm ashamed of it now, but I'd look at her and wonder to myself, what did she have that I didn't?

But ultimately, we all grew up. They ended up married and made a life in a small town in Alabama. I found the love of my life and moved to Atlanta, Georgia.

The years passed and I didn't think about him much. I had children, a career, and I was happy.

But life went sideways as my parents aged, and it got to the point where I needed to fly back to my hometown every Friday night after a long week of working, to go help my mom and dad deal with issues as their health was failing.

On one of those nights, exhausted and looking as tired as I felt, I arrived at the Atlanta airport and dragged myself all the way down the long terminal to the gate at the very end of the concourse where the plane for my flight was waiting.

And that's when I saw him. He was older and much heavier, but it was him.

He was 100 yards away, and it had been decades, but I knew that face. I'd spent way too long staring at his photo way back in my childhood to ever forget him. And there he was, sitting at my same gate, and that's when it hit me that I was looking far from my best. There was NO WAY I was going to let him see me again looking the way I looked in that moment, which was essentially like crap.

The sight of him somehow pumped some energy back into my body, and I ran to the bathroom, put on my makeup, did my hair, threw a breath mint in, and then, when I had myself together, I walked back out to that gate and intentionally walked right by him. I didn't even look his way. I made an excuse to talk to the gate agent, speaking loud enough that I was sure he could hear me, and then turned to sit down, fairly confident he would be paying attention at that point. And that's when I heard him say my name. My first and last name. Well, my old last name, from my youth, before I was married. The name I had when I spent hours staring at him each day.

My response to him saying my name?

Well, I waited a second, pretended to take a minute to recognize him, then acted surprised to see him again.

I know this is shallow, but that felt so good!

We sat and chatted 'til we boarded, catching up on all the years spent living different lives, and then, when we got on the plane, it turned out he was sitting right in front of me. And it turned into a weekly get-together, since he also had to fly out of Atlanta every Friday night to Dothan.

One week I even caught him snapping a photo of me on the Plane Train that takes people from the main security section to each terminal. He was definitely flirting and I was ok with that. He even posted the pic to social media where people actually confused me for his wife, who shares my same first name. He had to correct them that I was, indeed, NOT his wife.

Nope, he missed that boat.

And I couldn't have been more thankful. No part of me was interested in him anymore. I really did like the way my life had turned out, but have to admit, it sure was fun knowing I'd finally turned his head, even if it was decades after I wanted to.

All By Myself

LAS

Las Vegas Airport (overnight), Nevada, 2014
Shared by
Richard Dunn

Ever been stuck in an airport? How about all night? Well, it happened to Richard Dunn one night in 2014, when he got stuck on a last-minute layover. Instead of searching for a spot to sleep, he decided to take the time to get creative, and produce a music video, using his iPhone. And the result? It's spectacular. I'm not the only one who thinks so. It went viral, and led to even more fun for him, but I'll get to that in a minute.

If you have a phone or computer nearby and can google it, type in "All by Myself Richard Dunn". You'll be able to view the video that way.

If you can't, let me describe it for you.

Throughout the recording, Richard is lip syncing all the words to the Celine Dion hit song, "All By Myself", which is perfect, because that's exactly what it looked like in the airport that night. Totally empty.

The video jumps between shots from earlier in the day, when the monitors were full of flights arriving and departing, and people were making their way to their gates, to shots of everything emptied out, and the monitors completely blank, other than the time of 2:02am.

He got clever and set his camera up to show him all alone, sitting at the gate, then singing into the phone, even propping it up on an airport wheelchair, showing him sitting alone as the camera moves by. If you didn't know better, you'd think he had someone there with him to help, but that wasn't the case. He was just super creative. Throughout his video, he poses all over the airport, on a statue of a turtle, while riding the escalators, even sitting outside the women's bathroom. My favorite part is the scene toward the end, where he's reclined in a chair and splashes water on his face, à la "Flashdance" (a movie from the 80s, you have to see it to understand). He had fun with it. And so did we. And Richard says so did Celine Dion!

After Celine saw the video, and saw that about 11 million other people had viewed it in a few weeks, she invited me to come see her Vegas show (which was playing at the time I recorded the video) the next time I was "all by myself" at the airport. And you know what? I took her up on it! My family and I went and met her in her dressing room before her Vegas act, where she told me how much she loved the performance. She posed for pictures with us and encouraged me to keep making the videos from her songs.

Hey, as long as it's not the one from Titanic, where "my heart must go on" when the ship's outcome isn't good. That doesn't give off great vibes for ANY flight!

The Handkerchief

ORD TO CLT TO MCO

Chicago, Illinois, to Charlotte,
North Carolina, to Orlando, Florida, 2012
Shared by
Jennifer Rahaley

When most of us think of travel, we think of happy trips, heading off to fulfill dreams of seeing beautiful, faraway places.

But it's not always about that. Sometimes, travel is just a means to an end, a way to get to where we need to be.

And sometimes, that leads to a very sad place.

That was the kind of trip Jennifer Rahaley had to take in 2012, after getting a phone call carrying the dreaded news that her father wasn't doing well, and that she should get to him. As soon as she could. What happened on the way stays with her still.

I typically took a direct flight from her home in Chicago, Illinois, to my hometown in Vero Beach, Florida. But that day, the next flight available had a layover in Charlotte. I booked it and made the first leg of the journey, landing in North Carolina consumed with worry about whether I would get to my father in time. I decided to sit out my wait in a restaurant, trying to get through each hour, each minute, focusing on a glass of wine to help pass the time before my next flight.

I was struggling to keep it together, trying not to look like a total mess on the outside, but knowing I was doing a poor job of it.

That was confirmed when an older man, around the age of my father, kept looking over at me. The sadness was clearly winning in my battle to be anything but. After a few glances, the man eventually leaned over and asked if I was ok. The tears poured out. So, he offered me his handkerchief. Even joked that it was clean. That made me cry even more. You see, my dad always used handkerchiefs. And I felt so terribly far away from him at that moment, when all I wanted was to be by his side.

He told me he didn't mean to pry. Asked if I was ok. Asked if he could do anything.

"*After a few glances, the man eventually leaned over and asked if I was ok. The tears poured out. So, he offered me his handkerchief. Even joked that it was clean. That made me cry even more. You see, my dad always used handkerchiefs. And I felt so terribly far away from him at that moment, when all I wanted was to be by his side.*"

I explained to him there was nothing he could do. I told him I was on the way to the hospital, to see my dad, and things weren't looking very good for him.

His response?

"Well, tell me about your dad."

That was the magic medicine I needed to help me get through my endless layover. I started talking, and with each story about my father, I felt better and better. And before I knew it, it was time for my next flight.

I couldn't just give him back his handkerchief all wet with my tears, so I asked for his address so I could send it back to him once it was clean.

He told me no, keep it, but I couldn't let it go.

So, I asked for his phone number, anything, so I could reach him again later.

He finally relented, writing down his info.

Then I boarded my flight and went to be with my dad.

I got nine more precious days with him before he passed away.

And I still have the hanky, and keep it with me to this day, more than a decade later.

I did manage to find a box of nice handkerchiefs to send to him as a replacement, along with a thank you note letting him know how much his time with me that day helped me get through one of the worst times of my life.

And he wrote me a long letter back, saying how sorry he was for my loss, and as for replacing the hanky, he told me, "You didn't need to do that."

And he didn't need to be my angel that day, yet, without a doubt, he was.

Answer the Damn Phone

HNL TO STL TO TPA

Honolulu, Hawaii to St. Loui, Missouri,
to Tampa, Florida, 1994
Shared by
Barbara Bellay

I started surfing as a kid and got good fast. Really fast. In fact, I was on the professional tour at the age of 17, competing all over the world for the next several years.

Trips to Hawaii were common, since many surfing championships were held there, and in 1994, I was leaving Honolulu after competing in the Women's Triple Crown. My mom was traveling with me.

When we got to the airport, we were given the dreaded, "Sorry, your flight is going to be delayed, and we don't know for how long" speech. We figured we'd make the most of our time and head to the airport bar. There was a drink menu at their table, propped up like an A, with two sides. My mom told me to pick one side and she'd pick the other, and we'd order drinks until it was time to go. Well, my mom had her fill after just two, but I was determined to try each one, getting through the entire menu by the time our plane finally took off at 2am. My mom was tipsy, and I was beyond that, but we were on our way.

By the time we landed in St. Louis, I was feeling it. A hangover was starting to set in. And to make matters worse, our next flight was delayed, too. Something about an issue with a plane tire.

So, I attempted the impossible task of trying to make myself comfortable in the airplane chairs. Fortunately, this was before they installed the chairs that have those unmovable metal dividers between each one. In this case, they had what I can only describe as "crappy orange chairs that look like bent spoons". I sprawled out across three and tried to get some rest.

But the people around me weren't cooperating.

Two men, farmers in overalls, were talking about how excited their wives were about seeing Don Ho in concert, and how they didn't get it. One actually tried singing Don Ho's hit song, "Tiny Bubbles" which almost made me throw up (that may have also been the alcohol, but I digress).

I was sweating and sticking to the "crappy orange plastic seats" I was sprawled across. I admit it was gross, but a little better than the floor.

And to make matters worse, a phone kept ringing. Nonstop. For about two hours.

How do I know it was two hours? Keep reading.

Ring. Ring. Ring. Ring. Ring. Ring. Ring. Ring. Ring. Ring. Ring. Ring. Ring. Ring. Ring.

You get the picture. When I couldn't take another ring, I peeled my drooling face off the sticky seat, sat up and yelled, "Answer the damn phone!"

The flight crew had been standing there the entire time, ignoring it, until my angry demand. Finally, one picks up the phone, and I hear, "Oh. Two hours ago? I'll let them know."

I then hear him tell the rest of the crew, "Looks like the issue with the tires has been fixed, for two hours now!"

With the phone silent again, finally, I laid back down to stop the room from spinning and took another nap until it was time to board, an hour later.

Other passengers were thanking me for saying something, because there's no telling how much longer they would have been waiting for word that they didn't need to be waiting anymore.

But I was quite the sight. In fact, when I could only muster a nod back to one passenger who thanked me for speaking up, the lady commented that I must have suffered a stroke at some point in her life. But I wasn't partly paralyzed. I was just too exhausted to wipe the saliva from my lips or to say anything in response.

If you ask me what happened on the next flight back to Tampa, I couldn't tell you. I was asleep pretty much the entire way there.

The takeaway from this: Maybe don't drink the entire menu. And tell people to answer the phone much sooner.

I'll Be There

WPB TO MCO

to a rental car

West Palm Beach to Orlando,
to Birmingham, AL, Feb 1993
Shared by
Lisa & Jeff

Valentine's Day is just one of those holidays when being together is everything.

And when Jeff told his girlfriend Lisa that he was going to be with her for Valentine's, he meant it.

He probably didn't realize the lengths he'd have to go to in order to make it happen, but I'm not sure it would have mattered.

He had a mission, and he was going to see it through.

Lisa fills us in on his fortitude.

We'd only been dating for a few months at this point. We both had been working in finance, and had been assigned a client in Birmingham, Alabama. Both being from Florida, though different sides of the state, we'd flown home separately for the weekend, and planned to meet back up that Sunday night to celebrate the holiday together. I came in early, and Jeff was set to arrive by late afternoon.

But we weren't counting on a freak snowstorm that Sunday in Birmingham.

Jeff made his first flight, from West Palm to Orlando. But when he went to check in for the final leg to Birmingham, they announced his flight was canceled.

In fact, all flights were canceled into the city.

He was nearly 600 miles from me, on Valentine's Day, and there wasn't much he could do about it. And he wasn't the only one.

As people gathered around the gate realizing they were stuck, one man decided he was just going to rent a car and get there that way. Another guy jumped in, and said, "I'll go with you." And another. And then Jeff.

They didn't know each other at all, but they had a crappy rental car and eight hours ahead of them, and that was about to change.

This was decades ago, before everyone walked around with a cell phone in their pocket, so Jeff made a quick call to me and told me not to worry, he was going to get to me, though he would be late, but he'd definitely be there. And away this foursome went.

In the span of the next 600 miles, they certainly became more acquainted, and the holiday appeared to be saved for the guys who had girlfriends waiting in Alabama.

Right up until they got about two miles away from the apartments where Jeff and I were staying. It was late at night, the roads were terrible, and their rental car was never going to make it up the steep hill they had to go over to get to her front door.

So, Jeff, who had left warm, sunny South Florida that morning in jeans and tennis shoes, climbed out of the car, said farewell to his new friends, and started the bone-chilling walk in the snow to me, two miles away.

He shivered every step there, but finally made it to me right at midnight, covered in snow and frozen to his core.

Was it all worth it?

Well, that was 30 years ago.

Jeff and I ended up engaged about ten months later, and married the next year. And we've been married ever since.

Tests and Life Lessons

KEF TO JFK TO ATL

Keflavik, Iceland to New York City
to Atlanta, Georgia

You know how some trips are just destined to fail, no matter how much time, energy, and money you put into making them magical?

Well, that was the trip to Iceland I planned with my daughter her senior year of high school.

The snow outside the hut where
we were stuck in Iceland.

She loves snow, and I thought, why not spend one of our last holidays before college in a place where there's a ton of snow, but also things she would likely never see or experience any other way? Let's go make some memories!

So, when I saw a great airfare deal into Iceland from New York City, I figured why not grab it? Sure, we'd have to fly from Atlanta into NYC first, but for the difference I'd be saving on airfare doing that, about $500 per person, it just made sense.

I booked it, then booked some excursions I thought she'd never forget. The Blue Lagoon. Wetsuit snorkeling in a river where we could touch two continents at the same time. Snowmobiling across a glacier. And exploring inside an ice cave.

This trip was going to be epic!

Except I realized, after booking everything, that the school's winter break wasn't starting until December 23rd, not the 16th, like I thought. So, the week she'd now be missing of class was the week when most of her teachers were holding their final exams. Oops.

Any other year I wouldn't sweat it. She'd just take them the week she got back from break.

But in this case, she was applying for colleges that were waiting for fall grades to be submitted in order to make their final decision on whether to accept her. One college was her dream school. And they needed those grades before school was even starting back in January. She HAD to take the tests in December.

Yeah, I made a massive error in my planning. But the good news was we were scheduled to be gone Friday until Wednesday, so she'd make it back in time to take all the exams on Thursday and Friday. Not ideal, but I also didn't want to be out thousands of dollars, and the school principal understood my error (I was not alone in this; several other parents had emailed, saying they'd done the same).

So, that was the plan. We'd be cramming those exams from five days into two, but we were going, and making incredible memories.

At least that WAS the plan.

Day one went well. We had a red-eye flight, landed at the airport, and went directly to the Blue Lagoon, where we soaked for hours, letting the agony of the cramped flight dissolve in the warm, steamy waters.

We went to our hotel hours later, checked into our room, and made plans to head into Reykjavik, about 40 minutes away, the next day.

Except when we woke up and took our short shuttle to the 'bus hut' where we were being picked up about a mile away, back at the Blue Lagoon, there was a blizzard.

We were told it was the first snow the country had seen that winter, and it came down hard. And it didn't stop.

But we were in Iceland, so how bad could it be?

Well, bad enough that they shut down the roads. Bad enough that no car could come back to get us just a mile or so away, so we ended up having to walk that freezing cold brutal mile, in the blizzard, just to get back to a hotel where we could get food and eventually find warmth again.

And that's where we stayed. For days. The airport was shut down. The roads were shut down. Life was literally at a standstill. Who would have guessed?

Eventually, we were able to make it into the country's capital, but never did get to do the other excursions. No snorkeling between continents. No ice caves. No snowmobiles. We were lucky enough to see the Northern Lights, three nights straight, but by the third night my daughter was over all of it.

And then we were scheduled to fly home. But the airport had been shut down for days. Was it going to be open for us to fly out the following day? Or had I totally ruined my daughter's entire future, taking her on this trip to this frozen tundra, on the dates when she was supposed to be taking tests required for her to get into her dream school?!

Fortunately, that next morning we WERE able to get on the roads to get to the airport, and our flight was delayed, but still took off. It was a mini miracle.

I'd scheduled the New York to Atlanta flight for late in the evening, thinking delays were always possible, but in this case, we were still going to be sitting in NYC's JFK airport for about six hours. Those were hours she could be resting at home before the big tests, and I was desperate to do anything I could to get her home sooner, especially after the disappointing prior days we'd just been through.

So, off I went to the Delta customer service desk. I explained our entire depressing story to a fellow named Shaun-Chai at the Delta Priority Desk, with my daughter behind me the entire time, telling me to keep it to myself because she didn't think Shaun-Chai needed to hear my drama.

But when I finally finished talking, and spilling all the tea, so to speak, that man took pity on us and moved us up to the very next flight out, leaving less than an hour later. He couldn't promise us a seat, but he did put us at the very top of the standby list, and said odds were good we'd make it. I wanted to reach across the counter and kiss him right there! Finally, something was going very right on this trip where it felt like we'd taken every wrong turn from the start.

I told my daughter that sometimes it does help to lean on a kind person, especially if they have the ability to help.

We got on that flight, and got home hours before we were supposed to.

She went to school the next day, aced her exams, and sent the scores off to the schools she'd applied to.

And about six weeks later, she got the email she'd worked her whole life for. Her acceptance to her dream school!

Thank goodness.

I still say we have that Delta agent to thank at least a little bit for his kindness that day.

It was all quite the ordeal, full of mistakes we could control and experiences we couldn't control. There's an important life lesson in that.

And a side note: She says she will never, and I mean never, return to Iceland (I differ from her there). Guess that goes to show that the memories you make can't always be the good kind.

Who Makes the Cut?

Shared by
Pilot Simon Burke

It happens all the time. You're at your gate, just waiting to board, and you hear on the intercom, "This flight is full today and we are looking for volunteers to take the next flight. If you're willing to be rebooked, please come see the gate agent as soon as possible."

People look around left and right, waiting to see who might bite. Personally, I like to wait until they start offering big bucks. The more overbooked the flight is, the more money they're likely to offer. But not every airline will do that, especially in Europe, according to Pilot Simon Burke.

I work for an airline that doesn't offer any incentive, so I hate it when there's an issue with overbooking. I dealt with it on one particular flight that was fully booked coming from Paris to Exeter, England. The issue was totally unexpected. The airline hadn't oversold its seats. The problem was a child had urinated on the seat on the flight before, which meant the next flight had one fewer seat we could use. Before allowing anyone to board, I asked the crew what to do, and who should get the boot.

The ground crew said the last person to check in would be the first one to go.

I hated that idea. Called it "rubbish" actually. I suggested they offer extra money, but was told the airline doesn't pay. But they came up with something else.

The person on the intercom in this case asked, "Would anyone here like one more night in Paris on our dime? We'll pay for your hotel and a meal voucher if you're willing to leave tomorrow instead."

And it worked! Two people found the idea "brilliant" and were happy to give up their seats.

Problem solved.

Sadly, overbooking is pretty common because many airlines want to make sure the plane is as full as possible. They sell more tickets in advance than there are seats on the plane, kind of gambling on the fact that someone who booked will change their mind on the day-of the flight.

If that doesn't happen, typically there are a few things the airline will take into account in deciding who won't get to make the flight.

Different carriers have different policies, but for the most part, they have policies in place that mean unaccompanied minors won't be bumped, and they avoid bumping families, too, because it presents issues trying to get all of them on the same flight again later. Typically, people who provide the most dollars to the airline are pretty well protected. If you're in the platinum elite club, it's likely you're safe to hold on to your seat.

Some make it simple, like Simon's airline suggested, and go with the very last person to check in. So, if you're one of those people who waits 'til the last minute to get on the plane, that might be something you want to change in the future.

Something else to keep in mind: If you get booted and end up on another flight, that next crew has nothing to do with it, so don't take it out on them, or you may end up booted off the flight for an entirely different reason.

Right Place, Right Time

ATL

to San Juan, PR,
March 1, 2024
Shared by Gloria Smith

Know that phrase, right place, right time?

That's exactly how the people taking the 12:27 pm Delta flight from Atlanta to San Juan, Puerto Rico, on March 1st, 2024, must have felt. Gloria Smith was one of them.

Courtesy: Delta and Virgin Voyages

When we got to our gate to board our flight, it was like a carnival all around us, with games and decorations for Virgin Voyages, a cruise line. Of course, we were all boarding a flight, not a cruise ship, so it didn't make much sense. Until Delta's Chief Communications Officer, Tim Mapes, got on the intercom and introduced Sir Richard Branson, the Founder of Virgin Group, which owns Virgin Voyages, a cruise line. He certainly upped the party atmosphere at the gate. They invited passengers and people just passing by to spin the wheel of prizes, packed with Delta and Virgin Atlantic flights, Virgin Hotel stays, a Virgin Voyages cruise, Delta Vacation packages, gift cards and other great swag. Plus, Branson is a celeb of sorts and it added to their excitement as we boarded. I didn't really have time for that and honestly just wanted to get on my flight, having no idea what was ahead.

When we were all at our seats, ready to take off, Branson also came on the plane and jumped on the plane's intercom, making an announcement that left us all stunned.

"Everybody on this plane, we are offering you a free cruise (we all erupt in applause). And, you can bring a friend (we yell even louder). And the staff (so now even the crew members are overjoyed!)."

He continues, "Have a wonderful time and a lovely flight and I hope you have a big smile the whole flight! See you soon!"

It's safe to say we were all incredibly happy the rest of the flight. The mood was energetic and soaring high, just like the plane.

I live in Puerto Rico and was in Atlanta on business, so it's an easy yes for me to be on that cruise!

It turns out Virgin was launching cruises on its newest ship, Resilient Lady, out of its new homeport of San Juan later in the year, and this was a publicity stunt to let everyone know all about it. Delta Air Lines has a partnership with

Virgin, offering flights from ATL to San Juan, so people can fly Delta down to Puerto Rico to easily get to the port and sail away on one of the cruises.

But back to the flight packed that day, we all felt like we'd won the golden ticket.

What a treat they all got as they sat there waiting for takeoff, right?! Here I am, thrilled to get extra Biscoff cookies whenever I take a Delta flight.

It truly was a case of being in the right place at the right time for these flyers, and future cruisers.

Honeymoon at the Airport

BOM TO GOI

Bombay, India, to Goa, India,
January 2002
Shared by
Nirasha Kumar

We all dream of places where we'll spend our honeymoon.

An exotic island maybe?

A European destination?

But odds are, spending your first night alone as a married couple sleeping together in the airport does NOT top your list.

And that wasn't the hope for Nirasha and Ramesh, either, who ended up doing just that.

We flew to India for our wedding with our respective families.

As typical with India, it was a large, lavish event, with a whole lot of people.

Even on the night of our wedding, we didn't have the chance to be alone.

The next morning, we needed to drop my sisters off at the airport to fly back home to South Africa, so we decided to do something romantic and spontaneous. We packed a bag with a few outfits and decided we'd book a spur of the moment flight of our own. We saw my sisters off on their flight, then went to the ticket counter to book a flight of our own. We asked the gal at the ticket counter what domestic flights were available, and we chose Goa. The only problem was that flight wasn't leaving until the next day, so we'd need to spend our first night alone as a married couple at the airport. Sadly, that meant there wouldn't be much sleeping, and what sleeping did happen, would only be in shifts. We took turns, leaning on each other, trying to make the other as comfortable as possible, for as long as possible.

In hindsight, I guess that's pretty symbolic of what was to come for the next several decades, and honestly, what marriage is as a whole for all of us.

CHAPTER FIVE

IN FLIGHT

Ladies and gentlemen, on behalf of the captain and crew, welcome aboard Flight 101. You can expect non-stop service to your final destination. Keep your seatbelts fastened because this ride may get bumpy, and put your portable devices in airplane mode as we will be offering in-flight entertainment the entire way. Just keep reading. And thank you for flying with us.

My Eternal Seatmate

GSP TO DFW

Greenville, South Carolina,
to Dallas, Texas, 2018
Shared by
Rebecca Heiss, PhD

Do you believe in fate? Karma maybe? This next story with Rebecca Heiss, PhD may have you believing in both.

I live in Greenville, South Carolina, but fly all over the country for speaking engagements, so I'm in and out of airports all the time.

On this particular morning in 2018, I'm waiting in line to board, and overhear a couple in front of me talking about their seat assignments and how disappointed they are that their seats are separated.

Well, it turns out I have a seat next to one of them, so I offer to switch, so they can sit together.

They jump on the offer.

I get to my new seat and it's like I won the lottery–the seat next to mine is empty!

Good karma for the win! Please let it stay empty. Please let it stay empty.

Well, just before the door to the plane closes, one last person gets on the flight.

And he walks right up to "my" empty seat.

I knew it was too good to be true.

Well, at least he's cute. Too bad I'm not looking my best. I mean, 6 am flights, right?

He starts talking to me.

And it turns out he's got an accent *(who doesn't love a guy with a great accent?)*, which makes it much more tolerable to be having a full-on conversation this early in the morning.

He keeps talking.

And keeps talking.

And I'm actually enjoying his company.

Our flight is landing in Dallas, but we're both headed to different places after that.

He's off to Kansas City to meet up with other veterinarians (*hey, a doctor! That's the third check in the positive column, if you're counting)*.

I tell him I'm headed to California for a speaking engagement.

The conversation keeps flowing, and after a bit, this cute Irishman asks me out to dinner! And as crazy as it sounds, I agree, mostly because I'm impressed with his guts for asking. I mean, we're only halfway through the flight, and what if I said no? He'd have to sit next to me in awkward rejection the whole rest of the way.

Our flight is over fast, and I have to say goodbye to my sweet seatmate. We agree we'll have dinner whenever we both get back to Greenville, and swap phone numbers so we can connect again later.

My layover is quick in Dallas, so I'm up out of my seat and racing to my next gate, afraid I'll miss my connection.

I make it to the gate, drenched in sweat…and find out my flight is delayed 20 minutes.

Phew! Now I can catch my breath.

But I'm still thinking of the Irishman, so I send off a text letting him know I'd made the flight, now with time to spare.

He replies back immediately.

Irishman: Tell me what terminal you're in.

I answer.

Irishman: Stay right there!

Then, in no time, he's there in front of me!

He grabs me, right there in front of the gate, wraps me in a hug and gives me one great kiss!

Oh. My. Word. What a way to send me off with a smile!

> "*The conversation keeps flowing, and after a bit, this cute Irishman asks me out to dinner! And as crazy as it sounds, I agree, mostly because I'm impressed with his guts for asking. I mean, we're only halfway through the flight, and what if I said no? He'd have to sit next to me in awkward rejection the whole rest of the way.*"

We both go on with our trips, then meet up a couple days later for our dinner in Greenville.

And we KEEP meeting up.

We start taking trips together and grow closer and closer.

And six months to the day we met, he had us boarding a flight, the same exact route and time to Dallas, and the same exact seats! And during that flight, he slid me a gift across the tray table. An engagement ring!

He told me later that he'd bought that ring and those airplane tickets ONE DAY after we met! He was that sure I was his person, his eternal seatmate.

We got married a year later, and have been married for five and a half years already. And when we board flights now, people often ask if we're on our honeymoon. We tell them we are…because we now feel like our lives together are a permanent honeymoon.

Elainegate and Emergency Wine

BUR TO SEA

Burbank, California, to Seattle, Washington,
November 2019
Written by
January Gordon Ornellas

Flight 170 from Burbank to Seattle had trouble written all over it.

"Folks, it appears there is a significant storm developing," the ticket agent announced. We're going to board immediately, in order to beat the storm.

I sure hope we win.

As promised, my husband and I were quickly herded onto the plane.

The next announcement came from the captain.

This initial introduction is important. The captain's calm demeanor is what puts the passengers at ease.

"Uh, yeah … hey, so umm … well …" he trailed off.

I said calm, not stoned.

"So, yeah … there seems to be, um, a situation …"

This was followed by silence.

Were we supposed to guess the situation?

After a long pause, Captain Spicoli continued, "Um, because of the high winds and short runway, uh … We're not able to take off (longer pause) … the plane is a little …"

And that was it.

I don't know what was more concerning, the short runway, the high winds, or the fact that our captain couldn't form complete sentences.

The plane is a little...?

20 minutes later we got our answer.

"So, uh... the plane is a little... heavy."

We waited 20 minutes for "heavy?"

"Uh...we're going to dump some fuel, and um...recalculate the numbers," the captain said. "We don't want to kick anybody off because of, um... the weight."

Was he serious?

Was there a scale on board?

Why did I wear so many layers?

"

"So, yeah...there seems to be, um, a situation..."

This was followed by silence.

Were we supposed to guess the situation?

After a long pause, Captain Spicoli continued, "Um, because of the high winds and short runway, uh... We're not able to take off (longer pause)...the plane is a little..."

And that was it.

I don't know what was more concerning, the short runway, the high winds, or the fact that our captain couldn't form complete sentences.

"

On the upside, he knew the definition of "recalculate" and used it correctly in the sentence.

Ten minutes later, our captain announced some semi-good news.

"Uh, yeah… I think we're going to try and, um, take off."

TRY?

Let's lose the try. Just take off.

My telepathic motivational speech must have reached him because after some white knuckles, our supersize plane managed to depart from our undersized runway.

A little shaky at first, but then the winds calmed, the plane stopped swaying, and like an angel from heaven, something beautiful appeared:

BEVERAGE SERVICE!

Flight attendant Debby started in the front of the plane, and as passengers of row 29, we had a long wait. However, good things come to those who wait, and soon we were only 8 rows away… 6 rows… 3 rows.

Then, bump, rattle, whoosh! The plane rocked sideways, and before I could say Pinot Please, Flight Attendant Deby and her aluminum box of fun disappeared… and the captain reappeared.

"So, um, yeah, folks… we're hitting some turbulence."

Thank you Captain Obvious.

It was as if we were in a giant washing machine.

Windows rattled, tray tables thudded, lights flickered.

"This is bad," my husband commented.

Thank you Passenger Obvious.

I peered at the oxygen mask. I know it's there in case of emergency, and oxygen is a pretty nifty idea, but you know what would be even better… ?

Sippy cups of emergency wine that deploy from the ceiling.

It doesn't have to be fancy, just a house red, which drops into your lap.

Did I just invent something?

After half an hour of being tossed around mercilessly, the winds subsided and the plane leveled.

The lights came on, and the intercom crackled.

I braced myself for words of wisdom from Captain Spicoli, but this was a female voice, and she spoke in hushed tones.

"Elaine? Elaine?" she called. A few deep breaths before one final, "Elaine?"

Silence.

Was Elaine another flight attendant?

A passenger?

Were they summoning her from the great beyond?

The hairs on my arm stood up. It was like I was part of a supernatural airplane horror film.

Did I just invent a new genre?

Half an hour later, the flight took a turn for the better (aeronautical pun intended). Debby and her magical elixirs finally made it to the good people of row 29. "What will you have?" she asked.

Hmm, what pairs well with imminent death?

"Cab," I answered.

"Same," my husband said.

She wiped the sweat from her forehead. "I tell you, I'm not even a drinker, but after a night like this..."

That's not a phrase you want to hear from your flight attendant.

After filling our cups, my husband held his up.

"Here's to…" he started.

"A quick and painless death," I finished.

Cheers!

For the remainder of the flight, the turbulence lessened and we were able to enjoy our wine and dinner. And when I say dinner, I'm referring to my sad sack of reject pretzels.

As Debby refilled my water, I whispered, "Who's Elaine?"

"Tray tables up," she answered.

"Did you hear that?" I said to my husband.

"Yes, tray tables up."

"Not that. She ignored me when I asked about Elaine."

"Is it possible we heard it wrong?" he asked. "Maybe instead of *Elaine, Elaine,* they were saying, *the plane, the plane.*"

I digested this new information, nodding, "Like Tattoo, on Fantasy Island."

This flight had a lot of layers to it.

Twenty minutes later, our captain threw out some sentence fragments and we began nosediving.

So, I guessed that meant we were landing.

However, this landing felt more like one of those carnival rides, where you're freefalling from ridiculous heights, screaming in terror, and thinking, *why did I put my life in the hands of a carny?*

As we plummeted to our demise, all I could think was, *I wish that carny was our pilot.*

To say we came in hot was an understatement.

There were screeches and sparks and burning rubber. We may have lost a wheel.

The plane tilted to one side as we skidded along the runway.

I held my breath.

The skidding eventually slowed to a gentle lurching, then one final screech, and…

We stopped.

Along with the other passengers, we couldn't get off that plane fast enough.

Outside the cockpit, Flight Attendant Debs popped a Xanax and bid us good night.

Looking past Debs, I attempted to catch a glimpse of our pilot. I needed to know, who was this menace to the sky? And then I saw something: huddled in the corner of the cockpit was a small figure.

Was that a toddler?

Was this "Take Your Child to Work" day?

If so, well done, kid.

As I exited Flight 170, I pondered other questions:

Would "Elainegate" ever be solved?

Who can help me market SCEW (Sippy Cups of Emergency Wine)?

And most importantly:

Were our return trip tickets refundable?

Take a Seat

LAX TO JFK

Los Angeles, California, to
New York City, New York, early 2000s
Shared by
Todd Mazza

Many celebrities take private jets for flights, but quite often, they're cruising along mid-air flying commercial, along with the rest of us. That doesn't mean they want to be approached for autographs the entire flight. Many times, they'll do what they can to stay as inconspicuous as possible.

Courtesy: Facebook/Julianna Margulies

That was the case with a flight Todd Mazza was on in the early 2000s, as he explains here.

I was working for a major broadcast network and had to go back and forth between LA and NY quite a bit. That route is pretty common for celebrities, too, so it wasn't anything earth shattering if I happened to see a star or two in the airport, or even on my flight.

When I was checking in for this flight, I saw Julianna Margulies at the airport. At the time, she was a very recognizable face for her ongoing role in the TV hit series, ER, the show that launched not only her career, but that of George Clooney, Anthony Edwards, and many others. I didn't realize she'd be on my flight and didn't think about it again until I was sitting on the plane.

Juliana came on almost last, with special service directly to her seat, right next to me.

It was clear she wanted to be left alone, so I respected that. She was trying to sleep for most of the flight, but at one point, needed to get up to go to the restroom.

I offered to stand up and move out of her way, since she had the window seat and I was in the one on the aisle. But she declined, and just tried to move past me as I sat there.

We were seated in the bulkhead, where there's a wall instead of seats in front of us to grab onto, so she was using the wall to brace herself, but fell.

She ended up right in my lap!

We both laughed, then she apologized and got up.

No big deal at all, right?

Except to this day, it's one of my favorite flight memories.

Totally fair, Todd. Totally fair.

He Has Gum

ATL TO BOS

Atlanta, Georgia, to Boston, Massachusetts, 2005
Shared by
Sharon Renaud

When you have a family member who works enough hours for an airline, you are eligible for certain perks, including being able to fly for free, or at a deeply discounted rate. Sounds great, right? But the downside is you may not make it on the flight you want, and if you do, it's not always possible to sit together. No big deal if you're flying

Lilly Renaud, 5 years old

as a couple, but that can be complicated if you have children. So, families who fly what the airline calls "non-rev," short for non-revenue, understand they may be sitting at the airport for days waiting for a flight with available seats, and they teach their children to be self-sufficient if they're separated once they do get a plane.

The Renauds in Atlanta are one of those non-rev families, enjoying the perks, but also familiar with the non-fun side of flying standby. Sharon shared this story with me about one trip she took with her young children.

> *All the people around me were dying to see the little girl reunited with her mom. Maybe she would throw her arms around me and everyone could be so happy they helped out, right? But when the flight attendant got to me, he bent close and sort of whispered, "Um… she won't move. The boy next to her has gum."*

"As non-revs, our kids have been flying standby since birth. Sometimes, we are not able to sit together. When my daughter, Lilly, was five, I was traveling alone with her and Audrey, my then two-year-old. Audrey and I got seats together, but Lilly was seated dozens of rows ahead of us. I couldn't even see her. When the sweet flight attendant saw me buckling her seatbelt and reminding her to be good and quiet, he was taken aback and said, 'Oh no, this will not do.' He followed Audrey and me allll the way to the back of the plane and made a big, but polite, fuss, asking people to switch seats so my tiny girl could sit with her mommy. It took sevvvvveral minutes of everyone awkwardly getting up, moving back and forth, and everyone was so nice about it. I kept saying it wasn't necessary, and the more I protested, the more everyone's inner Grandma came out, telling me, 'Oh no, dear. It's no trouble to move!' Or, 'I don't mind at all!', and, 'I remember when my kids were that age! I'm happy to move!'

Finally, the flight attendant had all settled and a nice seat straight across the aisle from me. He went alllllll the way back up front and we could see him bent over a seat, speaking to someone.... like, for an excruciatingly long time. Then he stood up and walked alllllll the way back to me.

All the people around me were dying to see the little girl reunited with her mom. Maybe she would throw her arms around me, and everyone could be so happy they helped out, right? But when the flight attendant got to me, he bent close and sort of whispered, "Um... she won't move. The boy next to her has gum."

There was only a second of collective shock and silence, then uproarious laughter after that."

Sharon pointed out, travel is a worthwhile pursuit for many reasons. One great one is that it teaches us that, no matter where we go, folks are pretty much the same; we worry about our kids, we get annoyed with our husband, we are exhausted by our parents, yet, we are all usually willing to help out somebody else.

And she's right. And so is Lilly. A seat buddy willing to share his gum is much, much better than sitting next to mom.

The Scarlet Letter

BER TO IND

Berlin, Germany, to
Indianapolis, Indiana, 2010
Written by
Ginger Claremohr

On each flight, we only spend so much time with the people on the flight around us. And odds are, we'll never see them again. So, when our kids say things that make us hang our heads in shame, it's nice to know at least it'll be over soon. Just ask Ginger.

Several years ago, on a flight from Berlin to Indianapolis, my three-year-old daughter took a liking to the Italian woman sitting across from us. Fortunately, the woman also took a liking to her.

Initially, there was a bit of an accent barrier, but by the end of the nine-hour flight, they understood each other perfectly.

All of the passengers within earshot were amused when my daughter loudly introduced herself in a rapid succession of words.

"Hi! My name is Phoebe Allene Truitt. Phoebe makes a ffff sound, but it starts with a P. You make a P with a stick and kind of like a circle. This is my little brother Hudson Charles. Hudson Charles is two-years old. And that's my mommy. Her name is Ginger. Mommy has a husband AND a boyfriend!"

Smiles turned to frowns and a few passengers gave me full blown glares. I laughingly defended myself, "No, really, I don't have a husband and a boyfriend."

No one believed me.

A few days prior, Phoebe had been interested in learning about boyfriends, and asked me if I had one. I replied, "Daddy is my boyfriend."

"But he is your husband!"

"Yes, but before he was my husband, he was my boyfriend. And he still takes me on dates like a boyfriend."

My tarnished reputation did not improve when she announced, "We've been to Berlin to visit my daddy 'cause he works there. Now we are going back to the 'nited States."

I could see their minds processing; This woman's hard-working husband is out of the country, and she has a boyfriend back home. Those poor children!

For the remainder of the flight, I could feel the scarlet A burning into my chest.

Our trip involved a total of three layovers, the last being from Detroit to Indianapolis. We arrived in Detroit an hour late, and I scurried to get through customs, border protection, and security, so that I could pick up and recheck my luggage. Unfortunately, our stroller did not meet us there, so I worked my way through the airport with two wayward toddlers, two fifty pound bags, a portable playpen, three pieces of carry-on luggage, three jackets, AND a bag of wooden shoes I'd impulsively purchased on the Amsterdam layover.

It was exactly twenty hours from the time we got in the taxi in Berlin until we pulled into our driveway.

I cannot tell you how good home looked, even though the grass was overgrown, and I couldn't track down the unusual smell in the house. Now that I think about it, it would have been nice if my boyfriend had kept things up a little better while I was gone.

Can't Take My Eyes Off You

LAS TO LAX

Las Vegas, Nevada, to
Los Angeles, California, 2016
Shared by
Kate Clark

In the spring of 2016, I was leaving a weeklong industry trade show in Las Vegas where I had exhausted my last ounce of energy, meeting with media and influencers for a well-known baby gear brand. After wrapping up in Vegas, I was headed to another exciting series of work events in Los Angeles. Eager for some

Artie Schroeck, Kate Clark, Linda November

downtime, I arrived at the McCarran airport for the quick flight to LAX, looking forward to shutting down for that short flight. However, what happened after the descent turned out to be far better than a simple rest.

I settled into my first-class window seat and savored the quiet.

The white-haired gentleman sitting next to me was also quiet—perfect, I thought.

I closed my eyes, and before I knew it, we were landing. My seat neighbor began to exchange short pleasantries as the plane crawled across the tarmac to the gate.

"What brings you to L.A.?" he inquired.

I introduced myself, explained what I do, and shared that I had just finished one massive event and was on my way to another. Then, I turned the conversation over to him.

He introduced himself as "Arthur Schroeck," jokingly adding, "Just like the big green monster," but preferred to be called Artie, as his friends call him that. I found Artie, who was a few decades older than me, sweet and intriguing, so I asked him more about himself.

"Have you ever heard the song, 'Can't Take My Eyes Off of You'?" he asked in a quiet melodic voice. Upon my interest, he revealed, "I was the arranger and conductor of the recording!" His eyes twinkled as he recounted his dynamic career, including a long-time friendship with Frankie Vallie and memories of his time with members of the Rat Pack.

Artie continued to share more about himself. He mentioned living in Nevada with his wife but was visiting his son in L.A., who owned a bar and was hosting a big pay-per-view fight that night. He invited me to join, sharing his phone number so I could reach him. Artie also proudly shared that Linda, his wife, had sung jingles, including the famous voice of the cat from "Meow, meow, meow,

meow" Meow Mix commercials in the '80s. This made me chuckle because it took me right back to my childhood.

Artie's invitation to join him that night for the "big fight" was so genuine that, despite my exhaustion, I couldn't decline. I hinted I might attend after 7 pm, though I doubted my energy levels would permit it.

As the clock approached 7 pm, I was settled in my hotel room and my phone rang. It was Linda, Artie's wife, inquiring about my whereabouts, as Artie had been waiting for 45 minutes outside the bar for me. Never wanting to let anyone down, I quickly dialed up an Uber and was at the bar in 25 minutes.

That night turned out to be unforgettable. Artie and I hit it off so well that we became dear friends and have stayed in touch for the past eight years. He and Linda made time to see me in Charlotte when they came through town for a family funeral, and whenever I return to Vegas for the annual ABC Kids Expo, I make it a point to connect with Artie and Linda, whether in person or via social media and text. I enjoy hearing about their lives. They both live and love with full hearts, surrounded by friends and family. I especially enjoy the "pinch me" moments when he talks about his other son who is a talented guitarist for Kenny Loggins and Toto, as well as all the amazing memories he shares involving Frankie Vallie, and other big names who have entertained so many fans over the years. I've also had the pleasure of joining the couple for lunch at their home, where we sat close to one another in front of their Mac monitor and watched videos of them performing together on stage. They even showed me their "wall of fame," adorned with a Grammy award as well as photos of icons like Frank Sinatra and Tony Bennett if my mind serves me correctly.

This chance encounter blossomed into a cherished friendship, and I remain grateful for it to this day. I hope I was able to give Artie and Linda back at least an ounce of the joy they've filled my cup with. I'm certainly fortunate for these memories.

Michael's Mom

LAX TO ORD TO ORF

Los Angeles, California, to Chicago, Illinois,
to Norfolk, Virginia, late 1980's
Shared by
Paula Miller

Unless you're traveling with a few other people, when you board a plane, you really never know who is going to take the seat beside you. But sometimes, it really does pay to get a little chatty. It may just lead you to a story you can tell for decades, which is what happened to Paula on her way home from a flight to see friends in Los Angeles, as she tells us here.

As I boarded, I knew my husband, George, would take the window seat, and I'd be grabbing the middle one. We were ultimately flying to our home in Norfolk, Virginia, but had a layover in Chicago, Illinois.

We got to our seats and settled in for the flight, and not long later, a woman approached our aisle, sitting in the seat next to me. To this day, about four decades later, I remember the woman well; a very attractive Black woman, older than I was, wearing an olive green pantsuit and yellow scarf, and some of the most wonderful perfume I'd ever smelled.

The woman sat quietly, reading a magazine for a bit.

But then, at some point, the two of us struck up a conversation.

First, it was small talk, introducing ourselves and chatting back and forth about life; me sharing that I was a TV news reporter in Norfolk, Deloris (my new friend) telling me she was coming back from a Nike convention in LA.

She offers up that her son is a player in the NBA. I'm not a massive sports fan (other than my beloved Buffalo Bills), so the follow up questions are really just about being polite and keeping the conversation going.

I ask, "Oh really, what team does he play for?"

Deloris tells me, "Chicago."

So I ask, "What's his name?"

Her response, "Michael Jordan."

Did my jaw drop? No.

> *". . . at some point, the two of us struck up a conversation.*
>
> *First, it was small talk, introducing ourselves and chatting back and forth about life; me sharing that I was a TV news reporter in Norfolk, Deloris (my new friend) telling me she was coming back from a Nike convention in LA.*
>
> *She offers up that her son is a player in the NBA. I'm not a massive sports fan (other than my beloved Buffalo Bills), so the follow up questions are really just about being polite and keeping the conversation going.*
>
> *I ask, "Oh really, what team does he play for?"*
>
> *Deloris tells me, "Chicago."*
>
> *So I ask, "What's his name?"*
>
> *Her response, "Michael Jordan."*"

Remember, we all know who Michael Jordan is NOW, but at the time, he still wasn't a household name if you weren't a big basketball fan.

He'd signed with the Chicago Bulls in 1984, and got a shoe deal with Nike the same year, but not really following sports, I certainly didn't know who he was.

So I tell this sweet woman that I have to tell my husband, who is a big sports fan, but who's been in his own world while I was becoming besties with my seatmate.

I turn to George and tell him the woman I'm sitting next to has a son in the NBA. He doesn't seem fazed. He asks who, and I tell him, "Michael Jordan."

His eyes get wide, and without missing a beat, he looks down at the floor, looks up at her, and says, "Where are your Nikes?" Deloris erupts into laughter.

They get me up to speed on just how talented Michael Jordan really is.

We all keep chatting, now like dear old friends, and Deloris shares that Michael really loved *baseball as a kid, but he was so tall that the pants were always too short for him. He didn't like that, and everyone said with his height, he really should develop his basketball talents, instead.

We all know now that years later, he'd actually play both sports professionally, but basketball would become his legacy.

Deloris kept sharing little tidbits about her special son; nothing too insider, but all interesting. We became friendly enough that Deloris even invited us to her family home in North Carolina to visit one day.

It wasn't until decades later, when we saw the movie "Air" about Michael's Nike deal, just what a pivotal role Deloris played in helping Michael find success, on the court and in the business arena, too.

And even though we never did take her up on her offer to come visit, we certainly supported his Nike sponsorship, as we went on to have two children of our own, who both sported Nike gear throughout their own athletic careers. Plus, how fun is it that we bonded with the person who really helped seal the deal on Air Jordans, while all three of us were literally in the air?

A Delay Worth Waiting For

FRA TO ATL

Frankfurt, Germany to Atlanta, Georgia, 1989
Shared by
Tanya Naphier

Tanya Naphier was eager to board her flight from Frankfurt, Germany, to the U.S. in the late 80's. She was on leave from the Army, on her way home to see family in Florida, with a layover in Atlanta, Georgia. But her flight was taking forever to board. And she wasn't the only one who thought so, as she explains to us now, decades later.

Everyone around me was wondering why it was taking so very long to get on the plane and get it off the ground.

Not just that, but the airline wasn't letting people board the flight from the front of the plane, where we'd go by the first class seats on our way back to the main section. Instead, they had us entering the plane through a door farther back, behind first class.

But ultimately, I settled in, happy to be at my seat and ready for takeoff.

Not long after, I and the rest of the passengers figured out why it all took so long. There was a dignitary on the flight.

I looked up and saw none other than Former President Jimmy Carter (and a few Secret Service agents) walking down the aisle, shaking hands with anyone who expressed an interest. I exchanged pleasantries with the president, asking how he was and sharing how pleased I was to meet him.

"

But ultimately, I settled in, happy to be at my seat and ready for takeoff.

Not long after, I and the rest of the passengers figured out why it all took so long. There was a dignitary on the flight.

I looked up and saw none other than Former President Jimmy Carter (and a few Secret Service agents) walking down the aisle, shaking hands with anyone who expressed an interest. I exchanged pleasantries with the president, asking how he was and sharing how pleased I was to meet him.

"

I was pleasantly surprised to see someone who'd led the nation, flying the friendly skies, just like everyone else.

And it turns out that wasn't just a one-time thing.

Unlike most other former presidents who fly on private jets after being in office, Mr. Carter was still boarding commercial flights decades later, even taking selfies with many passengers (in Tanya's day, there weren't cameras in phones or she would have surely taken a pic with him). In 2018, more than thirty years after Tanya's flight, his spokesperson reported, he has shaken hands with travelers on planes for decades since leaving office and "enjoys it."

And you can bet Tanya enjoys being among the lucky few who had that honor.

The Day That Changed Everything

EWR TO DEN

Newark, New Jersey, to Denver, Colorado, September 11, 2001
Shared by
Peter Shankman

September 11, 2001, changed everything for the U.S., but nowhere was it felt more than it was in New York City, Peter Shankman's hometown. On this day, he was also on a flight. His just hadn't taken off yet.

I was sitting on the tarmac at Newark, buckled up in my seat, waiting for takeoff.

The pilot let us know our plane was third in line, just waiting for the two planes in front of us to get airborne.

We were getting antsy.

There was a delay of some sort.

The pilot came on the intercom and told us if we looked out the left side of the plane, we could see a small, black cloud of smoke.

"Word is a small plane hit the World Trade Center," he told us.

We strained to get a better view. A guy on my row muttered, "That's no small puff of smoke."

> *I was sitting on the tarmac at Newark, buckled up in my seat, waiting for takeoff.*
>
> *The pilot let us know our plane was third in line, just waiting for the two planes in front of us to get airborne.*
>
> *We were getting antsy.*
>
> *There was a delay of some sort.*
>
> *The pilot came on the intercom and told us if we looked out the left side of the plane, we could see a small, black cloud of smoke.*
>
> *"Word is a small plane hit the World Trade Center," he told us.*

The next thing we heard was the pilot, his tone drastically different.

"Sit down and put your seatbelts on! We're heading back to the gate," he stated with urgency.

And in seconds, we were making a hard turn and started hauling ass across the tarmac, racing to the terminal, going faster in a plane on the ground than I've ever gone, except for takeoff.

In no time, we were stopped at the gate.

We scrambled off the plane and had no idea what was happening until we saw CNN broadcasting in the airport.

By then, the airport was in chaos and the roads were shut down. We couldn't leave, so I grabbed one of the few remaining rooms at the Airport Marriott. Over the course of the day, more and more people ended up needing a place to sleep, and by the end of the night, we had five random women and one other guy sharing the space.

It was a long night, and the next day, we made our way out of the airport, then walked down the main road to try to hitch a ride with someone who could get us home. We managed to convince a guy with a pickup truck to load six of us up and take us to downtown Newark. From there, we took a PATH train back into the city.

What still stands out for me most from that day, September 12th, was coming out of Penn Station onto 8th Avenue, where it'd normally be jammed, and not seeing a car in site.

Then, turning and looking downtown at the skyline, to something drastically different than ever before. The city I grew up in was forever changed in a matter of hours. And so were all the people who called it home.

Do Not Worry. The Italian People Love the Americans

ATL TO FCO

Atlanta, Georgia, to Rome,
Italy, and

AUA TO JFK

Aruba to New York City, New York, 2001
Shared by
Lori, Flight Attendant

When 9/11 hit, the Federal Aviation Administration ordered all commercial aircraft still in the air to land at the nearest available airport immediately. Essentially, everyone was stuck in place for days, and no flights were allowed to take off again until September 14th. Lori was a flight attendant during that time, and the flights right after the incident still stick with her to this day.

I was fortunate not to have been working as a flight attendant on the day of the terror attacks, but I was on one of the first international flights trying to bring home passengers who'd been stuck for days. In this case, I was assigned a flight to Rome.

No one knew what to expect on these flights, and most people were rightfully terrified. But as a flight attendant, I knew I had to keep my cool, and try to be comforting to the passengers who weren't sure if their plane was going to land safely or be used as a weapon, like the ones on 9/11.

It wasn't until the plane actually touched down in Rome that everyone breathed a collective sigh of relief. Still, police met the aircraft, to make sure it was not dangerous, and the Rome station manager for the airline met them at the gate, kindly telling them in her thick Italian accent, "Do not worry. The Italian people love the Americans." I will always remember that, and how welcoming and comforting it felt to know much of the rest of the world understood our grief.

Our crew got a day to rest, then boarded a flight full of Americans who hadn't been able to come home. That was emotional, too, because these were people who'd been stuck abroad, watching their own country ache from afar. The flight landed in Atlanta with people crying, relieved to be back on American soil, safe and sound.

The next day, I was assigned a rescue flight to Aruba, to go pick up even more Americans who had not been able to return to their original destinations, because of all the grounded flights. That meant the crew took an empty plane into Aruba, then loaded it up with people eager to also return home, but in this case, their home was New York, the center of the destruction.

I realized we were landing one week to the day after the attacks, and as we approached JFK airport, every passenger on board was stunned to see the aerial view of the rubble of the Twin Towers, still smoking, as though the attacks had just taken place that day.

Sadly, flying into NYC would never feel the same for many Americans, even decades later.

The Book is Mightier than the Sword

BWI TO SFO

Dec 9, 2001, Baltimore, Maryland,
to San Francisco, California
Shared by Emilie Lorditch

Less than three months after September 11, 2001, Emilie wasn't thrilled about flying again, but work is work, and when you have to be at an event clear across the country, you have to deal with that anxiety and get back on the bike, or the plane, in this scenario. That doesn't mean you shouldn't still come up with an action plan for the "what if's".

I needed to get from Baltimore, Maryland, where I worked and lived, to a meeting in San Francisco, California.

It was December 9th, a few short months after the nation had come to a stop (9/11).

And people were skittish when they got on flights. It became more important than ever to look around at who else was boarding the plane, who might pose some kind of danger. Right or wrong, people were nervous and making assumptions. And coming up with game plans. That's what happened on my flight, but it was my seatmates who did the strategizing.

It was my first flight after 9/11. I had the new Harry Potter book, the *Philosopher's Stone*. It was thick. Hardback. And when I sat down in the window seat, a retired couple in their late 60s sat down in my row.

The wife turns to me and says, "If anything happens during the flight, I will throw my blanket over the bad guy's head and you can beat him with your book!"

I loved her for that.

Fortunately, we didn't need the book or the blanket on that flight, at least not used as a weapon.

Hey, you gotta use the weapons you have at hand, and if you've ever been hit with a book, especially a big, hardback one, you're well aware it'll stun you.

You know the phrase, "The pen is mightier than the sword"? Well, the book is mightier than the pen in this case.

Three Things

ELP TO DFW TO ORD

El Paso to Dallas, Texas, to Chicago, Illinois,
Sept 11, 2015
Shared by
James Coroy

Ever been in an air emergency where the oxygen masks drop from the ceiling and you aren't quite sure if you'll safely make it back on the ground again? Probably not, but it's not hard to imagine the fear the experience would trigger. James Coroy doesn't have to imagine.

On September 11th, I went through an emergency on a flight.

Not that September 11th. This one happened fourteen years later. But if you were around for the deadly attacks on the U.S., September 11th remained a rough day to fly for years. Many people avoided it, fearful of a repeat attack, as a "you never know if it could happen again" kind of concern.

So, when my wife and I were zipping along through the air on our 60-minute flight from El Paso to Dallas, a route I'd taken many times before over the years, I knew when something was wrong. I heard a loud whining noise, as if the engine was straining, and realized the nose started to angle downward. I turned to my wife and told her, "Something is not right." When I said the word "right", the masks dropped from above.

We slid our masks on, just as instructed in every pre-flight safety drill, then watched as one flight attendant froze up, paralyzed with panic. Another, more senior flight attendant, coached her through it, helping her keep it together, both of them wearing their masks as they dealt with it all. I watched as the younger flight attendant tried to reach the pilot, growing more anxious with each attempt and each unanswered call into the cockpit. I deduced the pilots also had masks on, and needed to focus on their emergency procedures instead of answering her call. They never did make an announcement about what was happening, or what to expect.

I saw passengers around me sobbing, some louder than others, and noted that EVERYONE was holding hands.

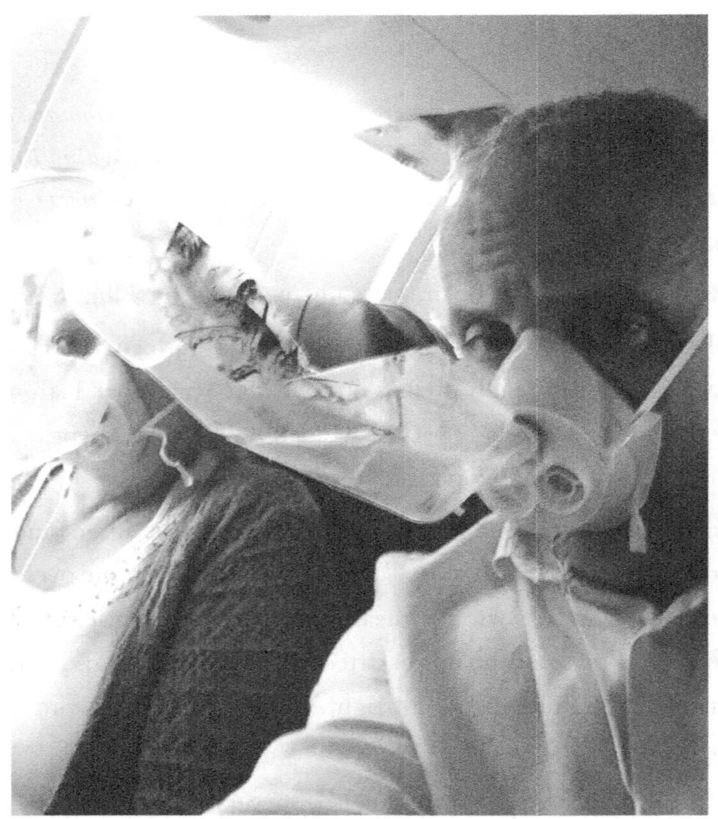

James and Angela Coroy during
their emergency, documenting the scare

As I witnessed this, I had three observations about what happens during an air emergency, when no one is certain if they'll survive. You do three things, not necessarily in this order:

1: You pray.

2: You try to call your family, likely not going to get an answer, but hoping you can record a voicemail with one last, "I love you."

3: You hold hands with the person next to you, regardless of race, gender, sexual orientation, or national origin. All of your phobias go out the window; that's it.

As I witnessed this, I had three observations about what happens during an air emergency, when no one is certain if they'll survive. You do three things, not necessarily in this order:

1: You pray.

2: You try to call your family, likely not going to get an answer, but hoping you can record a voicemail with one last, "I love you."

3: You hold hands with the person next to you, regardless of race, gender, sexual orientation, or national origin. All of your phobias go out the window; that's it. I believe you do those three things because that's all you CAN do.

On my terrifying ride, the plane dropped from 39,000 feet down to 10,000 feet, and by the time it finally landed, DFW went on full alert, a runway was cleared for emergency landing, and fire trucks, foam trucks, and all the emergency vehicles were waiting on the runway. The plane landed safely, and once ground personnel crews were certain there was no risk of fire or explosion, they ended up pulling up to the gate and let us get off, shaken but safe.

We later found out the plane had a blown pack. That meant the cabin was losing air and cabin pressure, slowly, but steadily, so the pilot brought the plane down to safer levels.

Frightening enough on its own, but having this happen on the anniversary of 9/11 took on a much deeper significance.

Fortunately, this time it had a very different outcome.

Mom Goes to Washington

DCA TO ATL

Washington, D.C., to Atlanta, Georgia
Shared by
Sharon Renaud

When Sharon and her husband were first married, before kids, they were eager to travel as much as they could, and since he worked for Delta Air Lines, they got to fly for free, along with family. So, they decided to treat her mother, Becky, to a trip to Washington, D.C., to show her all the famous sites and make memories together they knew would last a lifetime. They just thought they'd be making different memories than the ones they ended up creating.

Living in a small town all her life, my mom had only been on a plane once before, so this was a big deal for her.

The plan was for my mom to stay just a few days, and for my husband and me to remain in D.C. a bit longer. That meant we'd all fly together there, but then my mom would fly home on her own. That would involve a flight from D.C. to Atlanta, and then on to Tallahassee, Florida, which was just an hour or so from our small hometown. She'd have to navigate a connecting flight in Atlanta, but she was a smart lady, and we figured that would be easy enough. We even took some extra time on our flight out of Atlanta to D.C. to show her how to read the overhead monitors, to make sure she could find her gate later. We were a little concerned, but heck, if she'd navigated motherhood, getting around an airport couldn't be that hard, right?

Once in Washington, we got busy taking her everywhere she wanted to go. We ate at great restaurants and walked around the monuments, and even visited George Washington's home. After a few fantastic days together, we were back at the airport, putting her on a flight from D.C., to head home, where my dad would pick her up at the airport in Tallahassee later that day. Easy enough.

We exchanged hugs and went about our day. This was before cell phones were common, so later that night, when we figured she'd finally be back home, we called the house, to confirm she made it safe and sound. But nobody answered. And that was strange.

What nobody expected was a flight emergency, which is what happened on Mom's plane, minutes after takeoff. Something in the wheel assembly caught fire, and the plane needed to make an emergency landing. Fast. Instead of heading back to Reagan Washington National, the flight landed at Dulles, nearby. When it landed, the airline took everyone off the plane, made them get their luggage, and then bussed them back to Reagan.

When Mom got there, they needed her boarding pass to rebook her on a different plane, but she didn't have one. She explained that her son worked for Delta, and she had been walked onto the earlier plane by the gate agents. Again, she had no cell phone. She was essentially stranded and had no way to reach anyone for help.

Fortunately, another woman took mercy on her and helped get her back on a flight to Atlanta. When they landed at ATL, she even walked her to the connecting gate to Tallahassee. Then said goodbye.

But Mom was still a bit lost. Remember, she'd only flown once before and had no idea what she was supposed to do next, or when she was supposed to get on her plane.

At this point, miraculously, another person came to her rescue. This time, it was a massive young man who also happened to be flying to Tallahassee. He saw her and said, "Miss, you need to come with me," then let her know where to sit, and essentially stuck by her side, even sitting next to her on the plane, and then helping her get out of the airport. They talked the entire flight, as she told him all about her life, her children, and the tiny town where she lived in Georgia. He let her know he played football for Florida State University, which is why he was flying to Tallahassee. They couldn't have been more different, but on this day, he was her angel, the second one of the day, and she gave him a standing offer to come see her in her hometown any time he wanted.

When she finally arrived, her husband was waiting right there at the airport, not sure why her flight had taken longer, but glad to see her nonetheless.

And of course, my husband and I knew nothing of the wild ride her day turned into. But years later, it wasn't all the monuments or restaurants or even George Washington's home, but the journey home that ended up being the most memorable part of the trip.

Where'd He Go?

EWR TO BOG

Newark, New Jersey, to
Bogota, Columbia, 2007
Written by
Steven Lowell

These days, thanks to apps like Flight Aware, it's easy to keep up with a flight to see which gate it's departing from, whether it's on time, and more. But it's not always 100% current, or updated with information it doesn't have access to, which Steven Lowell learned about firsthand in the worst possible way. He also learned the young, male, All-American look might be great in the U.S., but not necessarily in other countries.

It's 2007, and I'm working for a tech company based out of Bogota, Colombia. I've just boarded a plane at Newark Airport, headed for my first visit down to the Latin America offices.

Everything seems normal.

About 30 minutes into the journey, the flight attendant is walking around handing out drinks and snacks. A young man in front of me is asked by the flight attendant if he'd like something to drink. And as he adjusts himself in the seat, something falls out of his pocket.

The flight attendant suddenly looks REALLY pissed off. And the young man in the seat just kind of nervously laughs. The flight attendant storms away.

About 30 seconds later, around 3:30 pm, the plane makes this huge 45-degree banking turn. We almost fall out of our seats. I hear a voice angrily announce we will be returning to Newark Airport.

The flight attendant comes back, asks the man to get up, and is walked to the front of the plane alongside another large man. I assume he's a flight marshal.

We get back to Newark around 4:15 pm, and as we leave the plane, we see the young man in handcuffs. He does NOT look happy.

We're all individually escorted off the plane, given our baggage back, and then security officers and dogs come through and search EACH individual bag. They open ALL of it.

We aren't allowed back on the plane unless we allow our bags to be fully searched.

Now, by the time we get back on the plane, 3 hours have passed. But there's a problem I'm not even aware of.

My wife is tracking my flight on a website the entire time. And she freaks out around 3:30 pm because the plane tracker suddenly says, "DELAYED" mid-flight.

So, she started calling my boss in Colombia. She thinks something has happened to the plane. This gets the entire company worked up because no one can find out what happened to the flight.

Fast forward, I get back on the plane, and finally get down to Colombia around 10:30 pm. But between getting off the flight and making it through customs and other various checkpoints, I'm stopped ELEVEN times by security, having my bag opened up each time and questioned.

My short journey through an airport ends up taking an hour!

I finally get out of the front doors of the gate.

Suddenly, a swarm of taxi drivers surround me! I'm physically being pulled in different directions by grown men aggressively saying, "Come with me! Come with me! I have a great car you like!!"

Now, by this point, it's pushing midnight. I'm falling over exhausted.

Suddenly, a strong arm grabs me and pulls me away from the cab drivers. A burly female Colombian police officer pulls me away, and the cabbies respectfully back off. They're clearly not going to mess with her.

She asks me, "What are you doing here?"

As I start to explain myself, my boss pulls up and politely says, "No worries. He is with me. Thank you."

I get in his car and two other colleagues are with him. EVERYONE looks like they just left a funeral. They're faces are filled with anguish, like they've been crying and finally found relief. Why?

Then they fill me in.

Apparently, no one had any idea what happened to my plane, so they were relieved to see me, safe and sound.

The young man who started all this was carrying drugs, which is why we were all searched. But they never told us that. Everyone at the airline kept saying, "The flight is delayed due to unforeseen circumstances."

The next morning at the office, exhausted, I found out all of my colleagues knew of my delayed flight for almost nine hours, and had been following it on a flight tracker app, just like my wife. So, when it was delayed with no explanation, and my wife had called them so concerned, they started thinking the worst.

The only reason my boss went to the airport?

He called the airline at 11 pm and found out the plane WAS safe, and had just landed.

But then I took forever to get out of the airport, which triggered new fears about what had become of me.

Unfortunately, that was the last time I was allowed to fly to Colombia alone.

I later found out that because I looked like a young college student from America, the police and airport security were on high alert, and did searches, thinking I may be carrying some form of drugs.

Understandable, given the fact that the fool who was caught on the plane looked very much like me.

The Not First Class Cat

ATL TO MXP

Atlanta, Georgia, to
Milan, Italy, 2002

As a flight attendant, Lori deals with all kinds of people. Sadly, many act entitled, and they're not always the ones you expect.

I was a pretty new flight attendant, working a flight from Atlanta to Milan, Italy.

I was getting things ready for the first class cabin area. The passengers in this section paid more and got more because of it. They each were given a nice pillow and blanket, left on their seat for their comfort later in flight.

Except, on this flight, after others had boarded and the plane was getting ready to depart, fellow flight attendants and I realized one pillow/blanket set was missing.

Fortunately, no one was upset about it, though it was definitely mysterious. How could it just vanish?

It wasn't until later in flight, as I was walking back through the coach section to get something, that the mystery was solved.

There, on the floor, was the first class pillow and blanket, sitting at a woman's feet. And perched on top of it, her furry cat!

I informed the woman her cat was required to be in its carrier, and tucked away under the seat in front of her. I pointed out that the pillow and blanket must have come from the first class section, where people had paid for them.

Was the woman embarrassed to be called out? Apologizing profusely?

Absolutely not!

In fact, her response to me was that she was an attorney from New York City, and if she was forced to put the cat in the carrier, she would be suing the airline.

Not the reaction I expected, especially since SHE was the one breaking the law, stealing something from the airline, then violating its published animal policy that she agreed to when boarding with the cat.

Of all the things I thought I'd be dealing with, a passenger with sticky fingers was NOT on my bingo card. But having done it for decades now, I know that you never know what each flight will bring.

Rushing the Cockpit… or the Restroom?

ORD TO DEN

Chicago, Illinois, to Denver, Colorado, 2004
Written by
Brooke Siem

If you're going to be escorted off a flight and potentially added to the "no fly" or "watch" list, at least have a really good reason. I believe Brooke's story qualifies. Keep reading.

For Thanksgiving break in 2004, I flew to my hometown of Reno, Nevada, from Middlebury College in Vermont, where I was a freshman. Flying between these two regional airports required multiple legs, including a two-hour Chicago to Denver haul followed by a quick Denver to Reno connection.

The movie *Love Actually* had come out on DVD (remember those?) and seeing as it was the start of the holidays, I was excited to settle into my seat at the back of the plane, put on my headphones, and shut out the hubbub of a long day of travel.

Sometime around Andrew Lincoln's poster confession of love to Kiera Knightly, I realized that my next connection was so tight, I might not have time to stop in the bathroom. The bathroom, which was positioned in the middle of Economy, was empty. We were also still surrounded by clouds, so I took off my headphones, put my laptop away, and rushed to the bathroom a few aisles in front of my seat.

Not long after I locked myself in the bathroom, someone started banging on the door. "Occupied!" I shouted, but the banging kept coming.

I washed my hands, opened the door, and was greeted by a short, animated flight attendant who demanded to see my boarding pass at a volume loud enough for everyone to hear.

This was 2004, remember. My boarding pass was paper and at my seat. He followed me to the back of the plane, took my boarding pass, looked at it, looked at me, and then *sprinted* to the front of the plane like it was the Olympic finals.

The guy sitting next to me was just as confused as I was. Neither one of us understood what was happening or why my boarding pass was relevant right before we landed.

The rest of the flight proceeded as usual. We landed, people shuffled off, and no one came to scold me, leading me to think that maybe whatever this was had blown over...until I saw the FAA agents waiting just outside the plane, complete with trench coats and badges.

I knew I'd done something wrong but didn't know what. As the flight attendant guided me off the plane, the FAA agents took me aside, and I noticed my seatmate hung back, too.

"I was making my final announcements for landing," the frazzled flight attendant spit out, gesturing wildly, "when she *blatantly* disregarded my demands, stood up and rushed the cockpit. I almost called a Level 4."

Level 4, I learn, is flight attendant speak for an "Attempted or actual breach of the flight crew compartment." It seems this attendant noted my swift scuttle to the bathroom and assumed the timing of my pit stop was about hijacking the plane rather than evacuating my bladder.

I burst into tears. I was 19, pigtailed, and about to go to prison.

"I saw the whole thing happen," my seatmate piped up from where he was standing on the jet bridge. He looked at the FAA agents and pointed to the flight attendant. "He was completely out of line."

The FAA agents nodded and dismissed both my seatmate and the flight attendant, who turned back to the plane in a huff. I got a talking to in the way a parent might talk to a kid if the parent had to save face but knew the kid didn't really screw up. Had the flight attendant called a Level 4, I would have been jailed. But since he didn't, I just needed to take my headphones out and listen to the flight attendants announcements from now on.

The FAA agents were required, though, to escort me to my next flight. And for the next seven or so years, I was regularly pulled aside by airport security, and every single piece of my luggage was searched. Not bad for a kid just trying to get home for the holidays, hoping for some love, actually along the way.

I Have to Go!

YHZ TO DTW TO ATL

Halifax, Nova Scotia, Canada, to
Detroit, Michigan, to Atlanta, Georgia, 2005
Shared by
Richard Dunn

If you fly a lot, it's likely you have enough reward miles to get upgraded quite a bit, but the person flying with you doesn't always get to move up, too. That happens often to Richard Dunn, who is in airports all the time for work. Typically, he lets his wife take the upgrade if she's traveling with him. So, when they were flying back from Canada in 2005 together and BOTH got upgraded, it was quite the treat. Until it wasn't, as he explains here.

My plan was to kick back with the extra leg room and enjoy the trip with my wife by my side.

And the plan was going smoothly, up until a flight attendant came on the plane's intercom, asking whether anyone on board spoke French.

As a Canadian, I took some French classes for a few years in elementary school. But that had been decades before, and I wasn't fluent by any means, so I kept my mouth shut.

A few minutes later, the flight attendant was back on, explaining they had an urgent situation and were pleading with anyone who could help to please speak up. I still stayed quiet, but my wife knew I might be able to help, so she raised her hand and pointed to me.

That's all the flight crew needed, so they asked me to come with them to the back of the plane where an incident was well underway.

What I saw when I left first class was a thin, older man pinning a much larger woman, likely about 300 pounds, against the side of the plane, as she was yelling, in French, "Je dois y aller!" I have to go! She was yelling it over and over.

I couldn't believe this man was keeping her from going to the restroom, so the flight attendant and I intervened, thinking the man was a real monster.

We got her away from this man and escorted her to the front of the plane, getting her safely to the restroom.

Then took a collective sigh of relief; tragedy averted.

Except, when she stepped out of the restroom, it clearly was not over.

She looked at the cockpit door, where the lead flight attendant was standing. She then turned to the exit door to the left, and a flight attendant was standing in front of it. Finally, she looked to the exit door to the right, which I was standing in front of, and she locked eyes with me.

In a split second, she was charging at me, and I weighed at least 100 pounds less than she did.

I thought it was bad enough that she was shoving me, but then she started reaching for the exit door, trying to get to the handle, still yelling, "Je dois y aller!" I have to go!

That's when it hit me! The man in the back wasn't the monster. He was trying to keep her from leaving through a door at the back of the plane. It now registered with me that what she was saying was that she needed to go out of the plane, which is not ideal mid-flight at 30,000 feet plus.

She was shoving me and reaching for the door, so I started pushing her face away, trying to say nice things to calm her down, but it wasn't working. It took several people to move her away and get her back in a seat, where we hoped she'd stay for the rest of the flight.

Fortunately, we were close to landing, and using the few words of French I could recall from my childhood, I was able to tell her we were almost there.

Sadly, not soon enough.

By the time we were cleared for final landing, she'd had enough. She appeared to be in a full-on panic attack, unbuckled her seat belt, and started shoving me, as I sat buckled in beside her. I essentially ended up in a wrestling match with the woman and had to unbuckle to keep from being crushed. I stood up to get a little leverage and the flight attendant jumped back on the intercom, insisting, "Mr. Dunn, you have to sit down! We're in our final descent!" I yelled back that I CAN'T sit, that I need help with her. The flight attendant ran back to help subdue her, and we both ended up having to brace ourselves through the landing while standing up, unbuckled, fighting back a woman pretty much out of her mind.

Ultimately, we did land and the woman, now aware she was safely on the ground, broke down bawling, thanking me for helping her survive the flight.

The rest of the passengers applauded, too, and the captain came out to explain that he had called ahead for a translator and security.

Only after we were on the ground did I feel I could finally take a breath, sad that I missed my relaxing first class ride next to his wife, but glad to have made it through without the plane having to be diverted for an emergency landing, which was a very real possibility in the thick of things. At least I was safely at my home airport in Atlanta, my wild travel day done.

But I couldn't help but think about the unfortunate part: Atlanta was just a layover for the woman and the man she was fighting with when I was called into action, who I later found out was her husband. They were from the islands, and the only way to finish their trip was by getting on at least one more flight.

Hopefully, she got a little help coping with going back up in the air.

The Celeb Seatmate

ATL TO DCA

Atlanta, Georgia, to Washington, D.C., 2015
By
Tyler Beckley

I was traveling to work an NBA Playoff game in Washington, D.C., and boarded my connection in ATL to DCA. I got the upgrade but walked on later in the boarding process and as I approached my seat, my seatmate was already in their seat. I informed them that I needed to get inside and they got up to allow

Courtesy: YouTube/WhiteHouse.Gov

me to get to my seat after placing my bags. As they stood up, I felt this air of familiarity come over me.

After getting settled I began the creepy process of trying to get another look at them so I could be sure, but all I could manage was a profile view of the face. Fortunately for me, the side I had a view of had a single mole that was in a spot that made it easy to verify, thanks to Google. After confirming it was indeed who I thought it was, I sent a few messages to friends as a "you'll never guess..." thought. I don't get star struck, so I make it a point not to bother them when I run into them.

We departed ATL and during the flight I pondered a way to break the ice once we landed, as a way to just let them know that I had seen and appreciated their work. Then it came to me, and I just had to wait for the right moment. I decided that I would wait until the last second to say something.

We hit the tarmac in D.C. and taxi to the gate. As the seatbelt sign turns off, I lean over and in a hushed tone ask "Are you here to put the p***y on the chainwax?" (In case you haven't figured out the celebrity yet, it was Keegan-Michael Key, half of the Key & Peele comedy team, and you'll have to do an online search of the chainwax routine). Getting a nice laugh from a comedian was cool! Leaning back over and in a hushed tone I hear, "No....I'm here to put the President on the chainwax!" We both laughed and then I was asked, "Did you hear the gate agent in Atlanta at boarding?" I told them no, I was late getting to the gate." They said, "Well, at the gate the gate agent recognized me and made an announcement over the P.A. asking, 'Would passenger A....A-RON. A....A-RON please check with the gate agent?', and I looked at the agent and gave him a smile and nod." So as it turns out, two different people at two different times had noticed him and given him and his work a nod. We wished each other safe travels and a good day and went on about our business.

I learned later that that evening was the White House Correspondents Dinner. Turns out that my seatmate was not only going to the dinner, but was going to be the most talked about moment from said dinner as "Angry Obama" (again, this is one you should search and watch…his Obama sketches are as good as it gets). Key was really gracious and kind to humor me and the gate agent for being a couple of fans, and I always thought it was pretty cool that we had the exchange that we did with his quick reply to my question, especially knowing just a few hours later he was standing behind Obama doing his Angry Obama bit.

The Lady Sitting Next to Me in Seat 13B

ATL

Flight to Atlanta, Georgia

As I approached seat 13B on my flight to Atlanta, I was happy when I saw the gal in the seat next to mine was a sweet-looking older woman. I was heading home to my family after a few days away and thought she'd make a nice person to talk with on the two-hour flight.

But, she didn't even acknowledge me when I sat down. I offered up a hello that I thought would break the ice.

Nothing.

She seemed annoyed, even at the kind flight attendant who went out of her way to get our trip started with smiles, despite the delay in departure. This flight attendant shared some silly riddles and got applause from the rest of the passengers. But not the lady beside me, who just shook her head, like she wanted to be anywhere else but on this flight.

I figured maybe this woman was just a grouch, and it certainly wasn't my place to try improving her demeanor, so when the door to the plane closed and nobody else sat in 13C, I slid over, figuring I'd prefer to have space between us instead of being inches from a mean person.

She could be miserable all by herself, I thought to myself.

So, imagine my shock when a few minutes later, she turned to me and shared her news.

> *I figured maybe this woman was just a grouch, and it certainly wasn't my place to try improving her demeanor, so when the door to the plane closed and nobody else sat in 13C, I slid over, figuring I'd prefer to have space between us instead of being inches from a mean person.*
>
> *She could be miserable all by herself, I thought to myself.*
>
> *So, imagine my shock when a few minutes later, she turned to me and shared her news.*
>
> *News that changed everything between us.*
>
> *"I lost my son this morning."*
>
> *Just like that. She said it. And her eyes said even more.*

News that changed everything between us.

"I lost my son this morning."

Just like that. She said it. And her eyes said even more.

I saw sadness that could have consumed the entire plane.

I know it consumed all of me.

"He was my soul mate," she went on to explain.

I unbuckled and slid back over to the seat next to her, putting my arm around her shoulders, holding a woman who went from meaning nothing to me to meaning everything.

A hundred questions filled my mind.

"How?"

"What happened?"

"How old was he?"

My mind was racing.

All I could ask her, though, was his name.

"Don," she answered.

I could tell just saying his name filled her with joy and heartache all in the same breath.

"Please tell me you have someone coming to meet you at the airport," I pleaded.

We were flying into Atlanta and that airport is massive. I didn't want her lost in the maze while her heart was clearly broken in two.

But Atlanta wasn't her final stop. She told me she was ultimately going to Indiana, where he lived, but just learning of his death, she had to go to Atlanta to get to Louisville, only to be picked up there and driven to Indiana.

The journey was going to be long. And hard.

"I never thought I'd be burying one of my own children," she explained.

She went on to share that she'd outlived her husband, her siblings, her in-laws, so many of the people she loved.

And now, her son.

"I've been operated on so many times," she continued, "I don't know why I'm still alive, except now, to be there for my daughter-in-law."

They were close, she shared.

She went on to explain that her son died suddenly, the day before, but no one could reach her until this morning. His death happened fast. He had complained shortly before of a headache. He simply went to stand and collapsed. Never to be revived.

His oldest child had died three years before from cancer. Now, his other three girls would have no father.

And his youngest, his son, would be graduating from high school tomorrow.

Tomorrow. And just yesterday, his father died.

The cruelty of it all crushed me.

And I never knew him.

But it wasn't hard to put myself in her shoes, and think about my oldest child, my son.

I told her how my son had just gone off to college the year before, and how I literally felt like I could not breathe when I had to leave him on that campus three and a half hours from home.

I told her how I missed him terribly every single day, how I desperately wanted to go to that campus and hug him every single morning.

And how happy I was when he came home for the summer. How it felt like my heart was whole again.

We both knew what the other was thinking at that moment.

Her heart would never be whole again.

She described her child as her soul mate, being born while her husband was serving in Korea. It was four months before the father and son met. This mother and son bond was tight. Like my own. And now, she was lost in sadness.

She pointed at her bag at her feet, explaining that it's all she packed and she had no idea what was in it, other than a nightshirt and a pair of shoes.

No one was with her on this flight.

She was alone in her sadness.

I hugged her some more, trying to offer comfort.

I wanted her to tell me more about him, hoping it would help somehow, but the tears were being replaced by numbness.

Talking didn't appear to be helping anymore.

And just like that, she turned to the window, staring at the world below, and at the same time, staring at nothing at all.

She didn't speak again the rest of the flight, and I didn't push it.

Instead, I thought about my own family, and how it must feel to have to bury so many others you love.

Less than three years ago, I lost my dad. I haven't been the same person since. I don't believe I ever will.

And I can honestly say I will never be the same person I was before being touched by this sweet old lady, sitting next to me in seat 13B.

Pilot in the Jump Seat

SLC TO ATL

Salt Lake City, Utah, to Atlanta, Georgia
Shared by
Sharon Renaud

One of the worst parts of flying standby as an airplane employee is when you're competing with tons of other people who have to rearrange travel plans, most commonly caused by flight cancellations and delays brought on with massive storms that make flying next to impossible. And that's the boat Sharon and her husband Kip were in when they were trying to fly back from Salt Lake City, Utah, to their home in Atlanta, Georgia.

A snowstorm in Chicago had shut things down there and there was a domino effect in airports around the country. Sharon and Kip were caught in that domino effect, making the best of a bad situation, as they share here.

We sat at the airport for three days straight, hoping and failing to get two seats on a plane to get home, even sleeping at the airport because so many other people were also stuck and had booked all the nearby hotel rooms.

They say three's the charm, and, miraculously, on the third day, we finally got a flight that wasn't packed full, and even though our seats weren't together, we were both on a flight to get home. Finally.

We boarded and sat at our seats, rows apart from each other, but thankful to be out of the airport and on a plane. I was sitting next to a kind, tall gentleman who was getting an earful about how happy I was to finally be on board, along with my hubby, even though we weren't sitting together.

All was finally back on track.

Or so it seemed.

Until a crew member came up to Kip and told him there was a mistake, and he was going to have to get off the plane so they could put a paying customer in the seat instead.

We both knew from past experience that it was always possible this could happen, and if it did, the other person was supposed to fly on without them, and we'd meet at the next airport whenever our other half did make it.

So, with this dismal but not totally unexpected news, Kip gathered his stuff to get off the plane and I told my seat buddy it looked like maybe our luck wasn't as good as we thought.

Imagine my surprise when the man stood up and told the flight crew that Kip could have his seat.

He explained that he was a pilot, and he could sit in the jump seat, something Kip wasn't allowed to do since that was reserved for only specific people on any flight, like a flight attendant, FAA crew, or a pilot.

It's not exactly a comfortable seat, so this was an incredibly kind thing for this pilot to offer, especially on a four-plus-hour long flight. It's a straight back, fold-down chair. Not ideal for five minutes, much less four hours. But he did it. We'll never know exactly why, but let's just chalk this up as our luck finally changing, after days of disappointment, and the kindness of a stranger.

Jetway Jesus

ISC AND HPN

St. Mary's Airport in Isles of Scilly, England, and Westchester County Airport in New York
Shared by
Pilot Simon Burke and Former Airport Manager Peter Scherrer

In the U.K., people with disabilities on flights are referred to as PRMs, or passengers with reduced mobility. And those who need help get it, even in the smaller airports, like the one in Isles of Scilly, England, where the firefighters are the crews called on to help transport people who can't get on or off the plane themselves. Pilot Simon Burke flew in and out of this airport regularly, and had one passenger he saw often who always needed assistance as a PRM. He tells us more about this passenger who turned out to be full of surprises.

The crew on this flight became familiar with this passenger, and had no idea what her malady was, but knew she could not stand, much less walk. Each flight, the firefighters would scoop her up and carry her back and forth to a wheelchair, so she could get around beyond the aircraft. So, imagine our shock when, after one flight, she was told the firefighters were busy, and she needed to sit tight for about 45 minutes until they could help. But instead of waiting, she stunned us all by standing up and walking right off the plane. She was magically cured! The crew looked at each other in disbelief, and deduced that what was actually going on was that she really, really liked having the strong, handsome firefighters wrap their arms around her and carry her away.

In the United States, airline crews typically refer to similar supernatural phenomena as 'miracle flights', and they happen often enough that they even give credit to 'Jetway Jesus'. I interviewed the manager of the Westchester County, NY, airport in 2012, for a television news segment, and he explained it did not go unnoticed that when 12-14 passengers per flight said they needed wheelchair assistance to get through security and board, quite often, once they landed, fewer than half still needed that wheelchair. Thus, the miracle flight moniker.

Orrrrrr, hear me out here, it could be people started gaming the system, knowing being in a wheelchair got you through the dreaded TSA security line quicker, and let you be among the first to board a plane. However, the perks end when the flight lands, and instead of being first off, people who need assistance typically have to wait until every other person has gotten off the flight. If you don't want to wait, and you really don't need the wheelchair, you get up and leave. And sadly, that's become much more common than most people think.

That aggravates people like Barb Likos, who has a son with a disability that requires a wheelchair. So, when able-bodied passengers abuse the system, it diverts the accommodations that he actually needs. She's an advocate for something like a disability card that is vetted, so only people who truly need a wheelchair are using them.

The airport manager I talked with pointed out the airlines can't legally ask a person what their disability is, and sometimes, it's not evident to others. If they don't provide the help, they can be fined tens of thousands of dollars, so it's not worth the risk, and is much easier to make a few more wheelchairs available, and have crews ready to push them.

The bottom line: The honor system rules the runway. And if miracles ARE happening mid-flight, here's a big salute to Jetway Jesus for making it happen!

On a Wing and a Prayer

LAX TO MXL

Los Angeles, California to
Mexicali, Mexico, 1992
Shared by
Charles Harris

Lots of people travel for work. And many of those people fly on private jets. But most of those people don't fly on private jets through severe weather, wondering if they're going to survive to see another day. Charles Harris, though, is one of those unlucky few, or lucky, depending on how you look at it. I'll let him elaborate on the fateful trip he took to Mexico in 1992.

As an executive with the Los Angeles Dodgers, I traveled with team manager Tommy Lasorda and a few others during winter baseball season. On this particular trip, we were off to Mexico to watch a prospect and future Hall of Famer named Mike Piazza. Lasorda wasn't just an interested coach, he was also a friend of the Piazza family, and wanted to see how the young player was progressing.

So, we were off for a quick, overnight trip.

We boarded the private jet. It was me, Tommy, the scout Mike Brito, and a few members of the press.

Business as usual, really.

But not long after we were airborne, we encountered a horrific thunderstorm, and things got rocky fast.

The plane was being hurled around in the wind like a rag doll, and the rain was coming down HARD.

I flew a lot at that point, and had been through some storms before, but nothing compared to that night.

I was sitting in the back, and it was all I could do to keep from throwing up on the beautiful tan leather seats all around me. It was like a roller coaster and I was white-knuckling the armrests the entire way.

It's not a long flight, but I was certain I was going to die that night. Honestly, I thought we all were. And all that kept going through my mind was "this plane is going to go down and the news is going to report on it, and they're going to say 'Tommy Lasorda died in a plane crash, with a few other people.'"

Shallow, yes, but honest.

Well, the fact that I am able to tell you about it now indicates we survived.

After that grueling, adrenaline-filled hour in the air, we eventually touched down, with a massive sense of relief washing over me.

We went on and watched Piazza play, and were hosted with a lavish Mexican meal, which my stomach still wasn't settled enough to be able to enjoy.

We knew when we saw Piazza that night that he was destined for the Major Leagues.

And we were not wrong. The next season he made the team and earned Rookie of the Year honors.

Ultimately, he was inducted into the Baseball Hall of Fame, so I guess it was worth the wild flight, though I'd never want to go through it again.

Blouse and Skirt

JFK TO JTR

New York City, New York, to Santorini, Greece, (with a diversion to Athens, Greece), April 4, 2023

Anyone who's ever boarded an airplane knows there are many, many things that can be out of the airline's control when it comes to getting you to your destination, and the biggest is the weather.

Even if your flight takes off and seems to be soaring along problem-free, sometimes, the surprise can come right at landing, and even if you spot your final destination just beyond your window, you still won't get to put your feet on the ground.

So close, yet so far. Santorini from our window.

That's what happened on my flight with my daughter to Santorini, Greece.

We dreamed about this trip.

I splurged and booked one of the top Airbnb spots on the island for our first two nights there. Knowing it was out of my budget for the rest of our five-night stay, I figured at least we could live the high-life for two nights.

That's what made it so much more devastating when, as we made our approach to the island, we started to hit major turbulence trying to land.

Our British Airways pilot went around once, and the plane would drop altitude suddenly, then recover… then it would happen again… but I thought we'd still touch down, until I realized we were getting farther from the airport, instead of closer. We started to circle the island and it was clear he'd aborted landing, but was going to try again. And he did. And it was a repeat of the first attempt.

For me, it felt like a carnival ride. You know, if you mentally tell yourself it'll all be ok, then it'll all be ok, right? Even if you're like kernels of popcorn bouncing around in the air.

The people around me on the flight did not have the same sentiment.

As our plane jerked up and down and sideways for a second, some of the other passengers started to lose it, literally.

There were prayers from some, curse words from others.

And then there was the exclamation of "blouse an skirt" I heard from the row behind me.

My mind didn't compute. Was she saying her blouse got under her skirt somehow? We were getting tossed around a bit, but not to the extent her skirt may have ended up over her shirt. What was she even saying?

Ultimately, I got my chance to ask her later, after the flight had been diverted to Athens, and British Airways had bussed us to a hotel for the night. While waiting in line to check in, I recognized the voices of the ladies who'd been sitting behind me on the flight. English accent, late 20's. Friendly enough looking. So, I had to ask.

"Pardon me, but were you the gals talking about your "Blouse and skirts" on the plane?"

They looked at each other and laughed. And then they educated me.

"What you heard me say was, 'Blouse an skirt', which doesn't mean anything to do with our clothing", Jasmine and Demi explained (yes, I did actually ask their names once we got talking).

They went on, "It's a common phrase in London. It essentially means, 'What the hell is happening here?!', or more crudely explained, 'What the f*ck?!'"

It turns out it's a Jamaican phrase that has caught on in London, and after hearing it on this flight, it's now one I turn to when I'm caught by surprise. And I always think of them and the flight.

In case you're wondering, the next day we were able to land at our dream destination of Santorini, though we sadly lost one of our nights on the island, including one of the two nights booked in the stunning Airbnb.

It was still worth every penny, and as with many trips, the unexpected made it even more memorable.

The Dolphins Fan

To Atlanta, Georgia
October 2015

The Miami Dolphins could never win another game and I'd consider them the best team in the league every single year because of what they are doing on the field today.

They're honoring a man who was just walking into the best of his life… serving his country, making his parents proud.

That was his goal. To make his parents proud. And he did, according to his father, a man I met on a recent flight.

It was a Southwest flight, so I got to pick where I sat once my number was called. By that point, many window seats were taken (my choice any time I get it), but there was one not too far back, with space above the seat to stow my rollaway. Plus, the guy who picked the aisle seat on that row was wearing a Miami Dolphins cap. Done deal. I knew he was my kind of people.

He had his laptop out and was taking care of business, so he seemed annoyed when I stopped him long enough to let me move by to the window, but gave me a smile when I told him I liked his hat. Immediately, we formed a bond.

I let him know I grew up a 'Fins fan and still cheered for the aqua and orange when they played.

I told him about my uncle, who named his dogs after the great player and Coach, Csonka and Shula, about my ex who grew up in Ohio, but as a child, pretended to be Marino, Duper and Clayton with his friends and was forever a Dolphins fan because of it. I told my new friend about how I treated my then-husband to tickets to the NFL Hall of Fame when Marino was inducted, along with our son.

And then, my new friend told me about his son.

About how they also were huge Dolphins fans, but lived in New Hampshire, so they typically only saw the Fins on the road. But he did get to bring his son to one game in SunLife Stadium—he'd planned it as a huge surprise. He described it all to me…landing at the airport and explaining they weren't going to visit his grandma in a nearby city as he'd said, but heading to a game to see their favorite team—in their home stadium. He walked me through the trip into the pro shop where they spent a bundle on all the fan gear they could never find back home. He shared that it was a real father and son super day—the kind you dream of having with your kids, with his only son—where it's all smiles and sunshine and memories to last a lifetime.

And the tears began to sneak out of his eyes as he shared just how happy he was to have had that time with him, because his son is now gone.

He died this past May. Just five months ago now. His father explained Cameron, it was the first time he used his name in the conversation, was only 26 years old, just launching his next step in life in his military career.

He'd just bought the orange (for the Dolphins) Jeep he'd always wanted. He was feeling good about everything about to come in his life.

And then he was gone.

Just like that.

Some of his military friends alerted the Miami Dolphins that they'd lost one of their biggest fans. The team sent aqua and orange roses to his funeral.

And not just that. They also invited Cameron's entire family to a game so that they could present him a military memorial on the field…the same field where his beloved Dolphins played their hearts out, where Cameron and his father cheered them on any given Sunday.

And that game is today. Cameron's father, his mother, his entire family, will be there to see this happen first hand. Honored guests of the team.

His dad explained to me on the flight that he wasn't sure how he'd be able to walk into the stadium again…where he and his son found so much happiness… where he'd never be able to take his son again. I know he'd exchange any on-field honor in a heartbeat just to hold his son again. But that can't happen. So, he'll hope to hold it together through the game, and hopefully find some joy in the moment for his son.

We hugged as I left the plane. Exchanged business cards. I knew I'd never forget him, or his son.

I'd give anything to be there to witness this with my new friend, but I know this moment isn't about me. It's about Cameron. And Cameron's family. And one amazing football team honoring its fans, even after they're gone.

Fins fans know there's a song that ends, "Miami Dolphins Number One!" All I can say is maybe not in the standings, but definitely when it comes to heart.

Coincidence?

LHR TO BOS

London to Boston, Massachusetts, and

ATL TO SJD

Atlanta, Georgia, to Cabo San Lucas, Mexico, 2018

Do you believe in coincidences? Or, are you more like me, inclined to think these serendipitous events are more than chance happenings in life?

Especially after a few recent 'coincidences', I'm in the camp with Deepak Chopra, who points them out as 'clues from the universe'.

In his 2003 book, Chopra explains "Coincidences are not accidents but signals from the universe which can guide us toward our true destiny."

I was reminded of this as I opened an email yesterday that caught me totally by surprise.

The subject line: Karlin, your seat neighbor from London to Boston

I instantly dove deep into my brain to recall my flight home from London to Boston last month. It was one of three legs in a very long day, which started that morning in Barcelona, Spain, and ultimately ended in Atlanta, Georgia, on the night before Thanksgiving (honestly, it ended up being the morning of, but let's not digress).

Anyway, I opened the email and the message inside left me in tears. Happy tears.

I'll let you read:

Hi Desiree!

I hope that your flight to Atlanta was smooth and that you have had a fantastic holiday season. Happy New Year!

I am unbelievably grateful that the Universe sat me next to you on that flight from London to Boston in November. What you told me really stuck with me – "when you have an idea, go for it, buy the domain, don't hesitate, don't wait, nail it down"!

Guess what I did the next day? I bought a domain! Not only that, I outlined an entire business plan for the business that I am now launching, piece by piece.

Thank you for sharing your knowledge (and armrest) with me. I will always be grateful.

Wishing you all the best,

Karlin

PS. How is "Be Good, Do Good, Find Good" coming along?

Immediately, the conversation, and Karlin's face, came rushing back. She was younger than me, probably in her mid 20's. We talked a bit about life. I mentioned my TV job, along with my websites. As a travel lover, she embraced the website idea, and told me she shared her photographs online with family and friends, but not really with the world. I encouraged her to make the leap, and gave her my business card in case she wanted to reach out later. I honestly didn't think I made that big an impression, so the email now—six weeks later–really hit my heart.

But here's the crazy part.

Her last name, which I don't remember her saying before, is Krishnaswami. It showed up in the 'from' portion of her email address.

The Krishna part is what jumped out at me.

Why?

Well, on a flight a few weeks after the Barcelona one, as I was making my way down to Cabo San Lucas, Mexico, I sat next to a woman who was incredibly upset. I was in a middle seat, and she was sitting at the window. She was trying hard to hold it in, but there was no way to ignore her tears, her entire body shaking with emotion. I don't know how anyone could witness that kind of hurt and not reach out, so I did.

I asked if there was something I could do for her. She wasn't able to speak. I put my hand on her hand and told her she didn't have to talk, but I wanted her to know someone cared. That she could take my hand off hers if she would prefer I leave her alone. Instead, she squeezed it. So I took it one step further, putting my arm around her in a hug of sorts. I let her know that the plane was safe, so if she was afraid of that, we'd be ok. If it was something more, she could tell me about it if she wanted me to know, and that I was a good listener. I told her I'd also been hurt deeply, and knew what it felt like to believe you were dying inside, or wish you were. To this, she gave me her eyes, and finally spoke, saying yes, that's what was happening with her. She explained that, as she sat next to me, her partner was in the back of the plane, choosing to be apart from her. She was crushed. We talked a little more, about big things like getting therapy, and about little things, like the jewelry she was wearing. She regained composure as she shared her belief about flowers—that they were smiles from God. I told her I agreed. I asked her name. Krishna, she said. She asked me mine. I told her. She smiled wide, then said of course I would be named Desiree, the same name as her little sister's best friend. She felt it was divine that I was seated next to her. There to help.

And by the time the flight landed, she was stronger. Perhaps even ok.

And now, a month after that last flight, this email appeared from my previous seat-mate, who turned out to also have Krishna in her name.

Two flights. To two very different parts of the world. Seated next to two very different people.

Coincidence? Much more.

And here I was, in the weeks after both flights, looking for direction of my own. Feeling a little lost, and honestly, a bit sad, about what comes next in my life. My marriage now over and family very different today than it was a year ago, I was struggling. Yes, I'd been feeling stronger and even hopeful for a few months, but as sometimes happens to the best of us, the hope started losing to loneliness, and my mind's fear over what was ahead for me was winning my daily battle for happiness.

While on the flight to London, I had told Karlin that during my trip to Barcelona, I'd bought the domain name for a new website I wanted to create: Be Good, Do Good, Find Good. It came to me while having drinks with my sweet friend who was hosting me on the trip. It felt like an epiphany at the time. It may have been the cava she'd introduced me to (again–the irony–cava is a Spanish drink, similar to my beloved Prosecco, pronounced very much like Cabo, my destination weeks later). Karlin had even asked about it in her PS in her email.

Yet, I'd done little more than think about that site in the weeks since purchasing its domain. I knew I wanted to put more good out in the world, but wasn't putting the work in to make it happen.

And here, thanks to what some would call coincidence– two Krishna's in my life, I believe the universe is sending me a signal, pushing me—hard—to keep putting good in the world, any way I can.

The TSwift Trend Before TSwift

CMH TO MCO

Columbus, Ohio, to Orlando, Florida
Shared by
Jan Hickel, Flight Attendant

Anyone who knows anything about Taylor Swift knows how popular it is to make friendship bracelets to wear and swap at her concerts. It caught on partly because of her song "You're on Your Own, Kid", with the lyric, "So, make the friendship bracelets, take the moment and taste it."

Well, Jan has a bracelet that's priceless to her, made by a little girl about eight years old, and given to her on her very first trip as a flight attendant. I'll let her tell us more about how it came to be.

When the plane was taking off, they announced on the intercom that it was my first flight as I started my new dream job, traveling the country for a living.

I was doing what I'd been trained to do; making passengers comfortable and keeping them safe and loving every minute of it.

Some of the people I connected with included a mom and daughter who were making bracelets to help pass the time on the flight. When they saw how much I enjoyed my new gig, they gifted me with a specially-made piece of jewelry.

And I still have it to this day, many years later, complete with the very appropriate wings charm hanging on it. Even though I have much more expensive jewelry in my collection, few are more priceless than this homemade keepsake.

Footprints on Our Souls

SDA TO ATL

San Diego, California, to
Atlanta, Georgia, 2002
By
Fadra Nally

I mentioned it before but it's worth mentioning again. When I get on an airplane, if I'm traveling by myself, I put on figurative blinders and give off the "please don't talk to me" vibes. I *especially* do that when I have a long flight. God knows I don't want to get roped into a conversation that has no chance of ending for five hours.

The year was 2002, and I was traveling home from a quick work trip to San Diego. I had a long haul flight back to Atlanta and clearly remember sitting on the left side of the plane, last row, on the aisle. There was a woman sitting by the window. I sat down, made myself comfortable, opened a book, and quickly gave off those vibes.

She must have asked me a question and somehow a conversation started. It was innocent enough. She wasn't a Chatty Cathy looking to pass the time. We just seemed to hit it off. She was old enough to be my mother and yet our chit chat quickly turned to deep conversation.

As the flight ended, she gave me her card. She was an executive with CSX, the transportation company (e.g., trains). It struck me as unusual that this woman would be in such a male-dominated industry and I never forgot her. Her words were kind, wise, powerful, and inspiring. I don't remember exactly what she said. I just know that her conversation filled me with the light I needed.

I sent an email to her a few weeks later just to let her know how much I enjoyed meeting her and I saved the email exchange after all these years. It still warms my heart.

—Original Message—
From: Fadra Nally
Sent: Sunday, December 22, 2002, 7:58 PM
To: Sandy H.
Subject: Happy Holidays!

Sandy,

We met a few weeks ago on a flight from San Diego to Atlanta. Remember the chatty one beside you? It was a pleasure to talk to you and you made the flight go quickly (thank you!)

I just wanted to drop you a line to let you know you really made my day. I want to wish you and your family a wonderful, safe, and happy holiday season. Hope you get snow in Florida!

Fadra Nally

From: "Sandy H."
To: 'Fadra Nally'
Subject: RE: Happy Holidays!
Date: Mon, 23 Dec 2002 09:12:22 -0500

Fadra:

How could you think I could forget you. I enjoyed our conversation so much! You are a beautiful, delightful and most interesting young woman whom I will always remember. I believe people come into our lives and some stay a long time, and others are with us ever so briefly but they leave footprints on our souls none the less. You are such a person in my life. I often wonder how God knows to send someone to meet a need that I do not even know I have.... that was you.

I wish you and your family a glorious holiday season and a most prosperous New Year! Unlike you... I hope we don't see snow for Christmas... however, they are calling for rain... and that could be worse for driving.

Sandy

Small actions sometimes impact others in a most unusual way.

Economy Class Syndrome

SAF TO DFW TO GSP

Santa Fe, New Mexico, to Dallas, Texas, to Greenville, South Carolina, January 2024
Shared by
Susan Smith

One of the worst parts of flying is all the sitting. In cramped quarters. For hours on end. They say you should get up every two hours to move your legs, but who really does that? And where exactly are you supposed to walk to? A restroom that you try very hard to never use?

Well, you might be rethinking that after hearing Susan Smith's story.

It was January 2024, and I had just driven my daughter 22 hours out to New Mexico to start her next travel nursing gig. I spent some time there with her, but needed to eventually get back home to South Carolina.

So, I booked a flight to Greenville. Having become a self-proclaimed plane snob in recent years, I typically took first class, to allow for more comfort on the plane, but for whatever reason, the airfare was through the roof for this particular flight, so I figured I'd be fine in the main cabin.

It was just one flight, so what was the harm?

I didn't know at that point that not only was I going to have to sit through several hours flying from Santa Fe to Dallas, and then even more from Dallas to Greenville, but I'd have an additional one and a half to two hours sitting on the runway in both locations, waiting to take off, thanks to lousy weather pretty much all over the country.

Somewhere on my way to Greenville from Dallas, I started to feel pain in my calf. I wrote it off as a charley horse, just a cramp in my leg. It kind of went away, while still kind of lingering. Not wanting to be a hypochondriac, I let it go.

But it hurt again the next day. And the next one. I mentioned it to my daughter, the nurse, who told me it could possibly be a deep vein thrombosis, or DVT. That's a blood clot that can form in your legs because you've been immobile for hours at a time, exactly what I went through on my flights. But I shrugged it off, saying I thought it was getting better, writing it off as a passing pain.

And that worked until a few days later, six days after my flight home, when my entire leg swelled up. That most certainly couldn't be dismissed.

I knew then I had to get to the emergency room, and I pretty much knew then I did have a DVT. The ER doc confirmed it, saying it was a classic case, telling me I "took a page out of my medical book." He did an ultrasound and saw several blood clots in my entire leg.

The doc added that they refer to DVT as "Economy Class Syndrome" because it may happen during or soon after a cramped flight. Look it up. He wasn't lying.

I was fortunate the clots didn't lead to a pulmonary embolism, which blocks arteries and could have killed me.

Now, I'm on blood thinners. And I'm already flying again, but much more aware of the things we all need to do to make sure we don't end up with a DVT, or worse.

A few tips, if you don't want to end up like me: Be sure to get up and walk around every two hours. Just do it. Even if you're just walking in place if you really don't want to take a stroll back to the bathroom. The longer you're on a flight, the more at-risk you are and the more necessary it is to move.

If you can get the aisle seat, that helps a bit with the leg room. It probably helps make it easier to get up and walk around more often, too, to be honest. And try stretching your calf muscles while sitting by raising your toes with your heels on the ground, and vice versa.

You should also wear compression socks. No, they're not very sexy, but hey, if they keep you alive, they're worth it, right?

And if I had my way, flight attendants on longer flights would do what my ER doc said they do on Malaysian Airlines, encouraging everyone to stand up and do the macarena right there at their seats.

Dance party on a plane? I'd book that flight!

Brrrr Onboard

I can't board a flight without bringing a blanket on board, because I know I'm going to freeze if I don't. And the thin, flimsy ones the airline sometimes hands out will not cut it. I need something that covers me head to toe, and typically use one I can fold up into a pillow case when I'm getting on and off the plane. I've appealed to the flight attendants to please make things more comfortable, and some have even agreed and said they'd do what they could, but I know now they were just trying to pacify me.

That's because the airlines intentionally keep it cold.

Yep. They have a medical reason for it actually.

A study by ASTM International, formerly known as American Society for Testing and Materials, looked into the correlation between people fainting while in the air and the cabin pressure and temperature. The study revealed that people may faint more easily while flying. It's caused by hypoxia, which happens when the body tissue doesn't get enough oxygen. That's more common when warm temperatures combine with cabin pressure, and is fairly common in airline passengers. So, the idea is to keep temps chilly, just to be on the safe side. The airlines have their own standards for cabin temperature, but say the planes are typically kept between 71 and 75 degrees Fahrenheit. It probably feels colder because you're sitting idle, and have no way to move around to warm up, it feels colder. I know it feels at least ten degrees colder than that to me. The airlines also have different policies on who can adjust the thermostat, with many only allowing the pilot control based on where it's located, although newer planes are more likely to allow accessibility to flight attendants, too.

The Association of Flight Attendants has fought to standardize the temperatures, but the FAA hasn't agreed to that yet.

Until that changes, and the temperatures are not bone-chilling cold, I'll continue to bundle up when I fly the friendly, frigid skies.

No Smoking Zone

JFK TO IAD

New York, New York, to
Washington, D.C., late 1980s
Shared by
Paul Litwack

Airlines in the U.S. banned smoking on domestic flights shorter than two hours in 1988. Then, in 1990, they extended that ban to flights under six hours. Ten years later, in 2000, the no-smoking ban went into effect on ALL domestic and international flights. Before all that, there were actually non-smoking SECTIONS. I kid you not. Just ask Paul.

I was traveling on an Eastern Airlines shuttle from New York to D.C.

When checking in, they announced the No Smoking section was to be the left side of the cabin!

Yes, you read that right. The left side. Keep reading.

I (and many others) thought they were joking, until we boarded, to see it was real!

While many of us were upset, the crew members weren't interested in changing the seating plan.

Fortunately, it was a short flight.

I never flew Eastern again (as they went bankrupt in 1991, others stopped flying them too!).

Let's just file this under 'what were they thinking?!'

Have a Coke and a Shave

MAD TO LGA TO BWI

Madrid, Spain, to New York, New York,
to Baltimore, Maryland
By
John Branning

The Alhambra is one of the world's great wonders — a stunning series of structures in Grenada, Spain, that have stood for over a thousand years, with a rich and complex history and, in more recent times, serving as home to a breathtaking collection of priceless Muslim and Spanish artifacts. I can attest to this since I've visited the Alhambra.

Well, that last statement may be factual but isn't accurate — while I have been to the Alhambra, my recollection of that visit and the remainder of a week in Spain are rather flaccid. My junior high school Spanish Club joined forces with our high school counterparts, and a group of forty of us made the trip one summer. I'd had only a year of Spanish and despite good grades my vocabulary was limited largely to words for "soup", "ham" and "cheese"; describing the temperature, and naming various members of my immediate and extended family. I could haltingly offer to bring my *abuela* a bowl of *sopa* if it were *mucho frio* outside. But if I managed to get separated from my classmates in the midst of a street market in downtown Madrid and didn't know the way back to my hotel, it wouldn't do me much good to ask, "*¿Cómo está usted?*"

I've forgotten most of that visit, at least the parts with cultural significance, because I understood so little of what was being said by tour guides, natives, and even most of my travel mates who were both more proficient in the language, as well as being older, sophisticated high schoolers who wouldn't deign to speak with any of the middle-graders. Those of us with only one year of Spanish under our belts spent our time bullying one another and seeing how many profanities we could learn to say *en español.* What I do remember, quite clearly, was the flight home.

We flew in and out of Madrid on TAP, the Portuguese airline. On the day we came home, we boarded the plane, pulled away from the gate and then... sat on the tarmac for over an hour in cramped quarters with all of the electricity turned off. As a result, there was no air conditioning and the temperature inside the plane quickly approached 100 degrees. About ten minutes past the point where death was certain, the plane shuddered back to life and fresher air began to flow through the cabin as we taxied into position for takeoff.

After reaching our cruising altitude, the flight attendants began the beverage service. A starchly-uniformed woman asked our row what we wanted to drink: aisle seat, "[something]" — middle seat, "[something]" — me in the window seat, "I'll have a Coke, please." A few moments later she handed chilled refreshments to my two seat mates and... went on to start serving the next row.

"Excuse me!" I called out. "I asked for a Coke!" She didn't acknowledge me. Another attendant passed through the aisle, and I fruitlessly tried to get her attention. I sat there, parched and defeated. I had no idea how to get someone to bring me anything to drink and finally decided to visit the bathroom for a cup of water from the tiny sink. I also decided to cement my status as an international traveler by shaving on the plane.

Now, I was all of 14 years old at this time and only needed to shave about once every other week. But I thought if I had the opportunity to mention to some comely young lass in the terminal after landing, "I just flew in from Madrid; took a shave on the flight," while firmly stroking my stubble-free jawline, she would find me irresistible and I'd finally become the man I proclaimed I was the year before, at my Bar Mitzvah. I emerged from the bathroom with a slightly quenched thirst and a highly irritated face flecked with dripping red streaks.

While walking back to my seat, I noticed a receptacle holding comment cards, with text in Portuguese, Spanish, English, French and one more language I was fairly certain was Klingon. I picked up a card and once back in my seat provided an evaluation of the airline's services. I chose not to mention the narrow seats or tarmac sauna and instead focused on this concern: "I asked two times for a Coke and didn't get it." The card requested my name and flight number. Not realizing they were optional, I felt compelled to provide the information but, in an attempt to maintain anonymity, spelled my name backwards: NHOJ GNINNARB (to this day I still sometimes introduce myself in one-and-done situations as "Nuh-HODGE Guh-NINN-arb" and tell people, "It's Persian."). No sooner had I completed the survey and folded it in thirds than another flight attendant appeared (where was all this attention when I was thirsty?), who smiled and asked me in English if she could take the card. I handed it over, figuring it would go into the box I'd seen next to the display at the back of the plane.

Five minutes later, my beverage-skipping nemesis was marching up the aisle, waiving my comment card and repeatedly asking, "Are you this person? Are you this person?" Apparently, they'd checked against the flight manifest, and after failing to find anyone named "Gninnarb" had decided to shake down the entire plane full of passengers. As she approached my row, I meekly raised my hand and ratted myself out. "Why did you write this? Where are your parents?" she asked. I said I was on a school trip. "Where is your teacher?" I pointed toward the front of the plane where Mrs. Miller, my 9th-grade Spanish teacher and the trip's organizer, was sitting. The attendant stormed off, returning a minute later with my teacher in tow. "John, what did you *do?*" Mrs. Miller plaintively asked me. "You have really upset this woman!" I briefly explained my version of events. She ruefully shook her head and ordered me to apologize for my actions to the attendant, who had been standing behind her this whole time. I looked at the woman and mumbled, "I'm sorry." She engaged Mrs. Miller in a brief conversation, I think in Portuguese, and then they went their separate ways. No one explained, in English or otherwise, why she never brought me my drink. But as the attendant walked away, I heard her mutter, "Fifteen years I've been at this job and the first complaint I get is from some… kid!" Half an hour after this fiasco it was time for the meal service. One crew passed out the food and another followed with the beverage cart. I was handed a sandwich, apparently made from gristly goat meat, which I left untouched. Then came the drink and, of course, the same attendant was asking for beverage preferences. She worked her way to my row, queried my seat mates, and then looked at me with a lovely smile and asked what would I like to drink? I quickly said, "Nothing, thank you." She smiled for another second or two and then, ratcheting her grin into a rictus of condescension and hatred, screamed at me — "ARE YOU SURE??" I meekly nodded yes and turned my gaze out the window, briefly wishing the plane would crash so this ordeal could come to an end.

We landed a few hours later and rode a charter bus from the airport to our school parking lot, where our families were waiting to pick us up. I walked around the front of the car and tossed my suitcase into the backseat, diving in behind it, still smarting from the beverage humiliation. My mother turned around to look at me and asked, "Are you feeling OK? It looks like all the blood has drained from your face!" My dad eyed me in the rearview mirror, seeing my shaving scars, and promptly added, "… and apparently dripped down his neck."

Did I Just Dream That?

MYR TO CLT TO ATW

Myrtle Beach, South Carolina,
to Charlotte, North Carolina, to
Appleton, Wisconsin, October 2021
Shared by
Tommy Clifford

When you're flying late at night and really just want to go to sleep, nothing is better than getting a sweet first class seat on a flight. Well, maybe getting two, so your sweetheart can be right next to you. And that was the situation Tommy Clifford was in as he and his wife returned to Wisconsin after a getaway to Myrtle Beach, South Carolina. But he soon realized being in first class doesn't always make you immune from the crazy, as he tells us here.

We're in seats 1A and 1B, right up front.

When we boarded, I noticed a gentleman sitting behind us a couple rows, still in first class, wearing a hoodie and facemask (this was after the mask mandate was lifted, so not required, and not rare, but still noteworthy). To be honest, he was kind of giving off Unabomber vibes, but I wasn't too worried. It was the end of my trip and I just wanted to get home.

Well, we're halfway through the flight and the lights were dimmed, super peaceful on the plane. I've got my iPad out, AirPods in, and am delightfully dozing in and out.

Until I feel a thumb digging into my shoulder blade, from behind.

Then I hear a flight attendant say quietly, "He's peeing all over my partner."

That wakes me right up.

I see the door to the front lavatory wide open, with the man in the hoodie standing there, sweat pants down around his ankles, spraying the flight attendants.

I'm stunned, and wake my wife up.

"What the hell is going on?" we both ask, as if anyone can explain this absurdity.

> *Well, we're halfway through the flight and the lights were dimmed, super peaceful on the plane. I've got my iPad out, AirPods in, and am delightfully dozing in and out.*
>
> *Until I feel a thumb digging into my shoulder blade, from behind.*
>
> *Then I hear a flight attendant say quietly, "He's peeing all over my partner."*
>
> *That wakes me right up.*
>
> *I see the door to the front lavatory wide open, with the man in the hoodie standing there, sweat pants down around his ankles, spraying the flight attendants.*

Then he goes back in the bathroom and tries to close the door, but isn't able to make it connect, so it swings open again. He's taking care of business, so to speak.

The flight attendants are scrambling, trying to figure out how to handle the peeing passenger. They're on the phone with the pilot. Then they're on the floor with towels, wiping up what they can see in the dark.

Then, suddenly, he pulls up his pants and leaves the bathroom, stumbles to his seat, puts his hood up over his head, mask back on, and hands in his pockets.

And proceeds to fall right back asleep.

I tell my wife I promise there will be police when we land, and sure enough, once we're back on the ground, the flight attendants command us to keep our seats. And I can see on the tarmac there's a sheriff's car and medical crews.

It's after midnight and we just want to get home.

Finally, we're allowed to leave the plane, and even though we're the first passengers off, I really wanted to stick around until the man walked off, to see what they were going to do with him.

Sure enough, he gets off, is pulled to the side, and they ask him, "Where are you going? What are you doing here?"

"I'm a travel nurse," he answers, "and I'm here for work."

That explains the mask.

But then I hear him saying, incredulously, "I did what?! There's NO way!"

He had no recollection at all of his antics on the airplane. Or, at least that was his story, and he was sticking to it.

So, was he sleepwalking? Was he deep in a dream? Or deeply medicated maybe?

To be honest, it all happened so fast, if I didn't have others to confirm what I saw, I would have thought I dreamt it myself.

Going Above and Beyond

BWI TO SAN

Baltimore, Maryland, to San Diego, California
Shared by a friend who is a
flight attendant (who asked to remain anonymous)

It was the holiday season, and this was my first Christmas working as a flight attendant. I was headed from Baltimore to San Diego, and we got in late. I remember it was the holidays because my fellow flight attendant was wearing holiday stockings and antlers on her head.

As we were wrapping up everything on the plane, she popped her head into the lavatory (restroom) and came out screaming!

There was one lonely turd on the floor by the toilet.

No streak that it was even close to making it to the target.

No one had been in there with diarrhea.

This was just one solid poop that didn't make it into the toilet, whether intentional or not.

We racked our brains to figure out who might have been in there last and left us their excrement. We nicknamed it "Poopgate", trying to remember who left the bathroom last, not that it mattered "in the end."

Someone had left us a gift for the holidays, and it was a gift we absolutely wanted to return.

Ultimately, my fellow flight attendant who discovered the disgusting token in the toilet grabbed some toilet paper and disposed of it properly.

This deserved a medal in my mind, so I made sure to write a note to our bosses about her extra effort going above and beyond "in the line of doody."

Pun intended.

That New Plane Smell

MUC TO ATL

Munich, Germany, to Atlanta, Georgia
Shared by
Lori, Flight Attendant

Brand new airplanes have a new plane smell, just like you find in a new car. It's a mixture of the leather and carpet and all the plastics that are part of the plane.

So, I was thrilled to be serving in the "purser" role on this flight, which was much like the chief flight attendant, making sure passengers were safe and comfortable, on a plane that was only two weeks old.

That is, I was thrilled right up until some of the passengers started complaining about a horrible stench.

Fellow flight attendants let me know there was a definite problem.

So, I went to investigate.

Standing in the aisle in the front section of the plane, just beyond first class, was a woman. I immediately wondered to myself if this woman had just had a major accident, because along the floor of the plane was a trail of diarrhea. The woman quickly exclaimed, "It's my dog!"

I sent her and her pungent pet to the restroom, then did my best to start eliminating the odor. This is the part of being a flight attendant that is anything but glorified. But, mid-air, someone has to deal with cleanups, and that duty fell to me on this trip.

After scrubbing away what I could, much of the stench remained, and passengers demanded they be moved, hoping to be separated from the stench. Think about it; it's not like anyone could just open a window.

The problem was, there were only so many empty seats. So, I did what I could to reassign who I could, but that ended up getting combative. Passengers were ready to punch each other over who got to move and who had to stay and suffer. They were yelling at the lady who brought the smelly putrid pet, arguing among each other, and taking all their frustrations out on us in the flight crew. At one point, it was so bad I thought I was going to have to divert the plane to an earlier stop, just to take the angry passengers off the flight, with some of them facing arrest if their behavior escalated.

By some miracle, we made it through to our final destination without having to add another stop, which never goes over well with anyone on board.

But you can bet they were all more than ready to leave as soon as that plane got to the gate. And I was ready for the flight to be over, too, right along with them.

Along Came a Spider

IAH TO DEN

Houston, TX, to Denver, CO
Shared by a friend who is a flight attendant
(who asked to remain anonymous)

A flight attendant never knows what to expect on any given flight, but odds are things in first class are less chaotic than the rest of the plane. At least that's usually the case.

Except on this particular flight, where the flight attendant in first class was brand new, though even someone who'd been flying for decades would have been shocked by this one.

In this case, a woman had gone into the lavatory (restroom) by the front galley. After about a minute, I heard a massive ruckus, with things banging against the door. Before I knew it, a woman threw open the door, her panties down around her ankles, though fortunately she had on a long shirt dress, so most of her was covered. She yelled, "There's a spider in there!"

Well, alrighty then.

She got back to her aisle and pulled up her panties before taking a seat.

I went into the bathroom to try to take care of said spider, but it was nowhere to be found.

Was there one?

Hard to say. Maybe it was actually in the toilet, and ended up flushed out into the ether.

"

a woman had gone into the lavatory (restroom) by the front galley. After about a minute, I heard a massive ruckus, with things banging against the door. Before I knew it, a woman threw open the door, her panties down around her ankles, though fortunately she had on a long shirt dress, so most of her was covered. She yelled, "There's a spider in there!"

"

Or, maybe he made a quick exit, just like the lady did, once she flung open the door to make her escape.

All we know is there's a whole new version of Little Miss Muffett, on a toilet instead of a tuffet, where along came a spider, who sat down beside her, scaring Miss Muffett away.

Face-to-Face Flight

ATL TO ORD TO LHR

Atlanta, Georgia, to Chicago, Illinois,
to London, England, November 2009

With the advent of video conferencing in the early 2000's, some airlines started to take notice that it was really making a dent in their business travel. After all, why bother spending the time and money flying back and forth either cross-country or even across the pond to do business, when you could see each other through a computer screen and make deals happen instantly?

Except one airline, British Airways, argued the computer screen was not at all the same, and that you could build better relationships, and thus, better business, by working together face-to-face.

So, the airline launched a contest.

They called it the British Airways new Face-to-Face program and offered entrepreneurs free tickets anywhere in the world where it flies. But before going off to anywhere, the small business owners would fly out of Chicago, LA, or NYC, to London, for a few days of meetings on how to grow their business.

Well, when this contest launched in 2009, I'd just started a business of my own and hadn't even landed a client, but I liked the sound of a free flight to anywhere, along with some business advice, so I spent about five minutes submitting a response to their contest question about my company and how it might help to be able to grow it overseas.

Imagine my surprise when, a few weeks later, I got a phone call saying I was one of the winners! I thought I was being pranked, or the 2009 hip term for it was punked, so I told them to give me their phone number so I could call them back and make sure it was legit. Again, I was stunned when their phone rang and the same man answered, laughing at my skeptical reaction to winning. The call was followed up by an email, and in a matter of weeks, I was part of this batch of winners set to fly out of Chicago for this incredible opportunity.

There was a big, catered sendoff reception for us in a private room at the airport, along with the mayor of Chicago, Richard Daley, and London's mayor, Boris Johnson. There were about 200 of us and I wasn't the only one in disbelief about our good fortune.

After the gathering, they had us board a plane, but not just any plane. It was a Boeing 747-400 charter that was waiting to whisk us away across the pond. It was painted with the words "Face-to-Face" and we took our seats for takeoff, but that's the only time we were required to sit until landing. The rest of the flight was extremely social, with the crew making it clear we could move around the cabin at will, networking nearly every minute of the flight. The fellow sitting next to me was an expert at franchising, and explained how simple it would be to franchise my business idea once I got it rolling. Again, I didn't even have my first customer yet, but already had some pretty important people believing in the business enough to get me going on an international scale.

There are few flights where so many people WANT to get to know the person in the seat beside them, much less the rest of the plane, but that wasn't the case here. Everyone was eager to make connections, knowing each person had something significant to offer others, at least when it came to entrepreneurship.

The overnight flight ended all too soon in this case, and when it landed at Heathrow, we knew the next couple days were going to be life-changing.

We weren't wrong. We got guidance from Lords and Knights, and Olympic gold medal-winning coaches, on how to build teams and ways to make our businesses work. They even threw us a party at the Orangery at Kensington Palace, the home Princess Diana had lived in just years before.

After my time in London, I took my free flight to Greece, picked mainly because I'd just watched the movie "Mamma Mia" and really wanted to see the beautiful location where it was filmed. Probably not what British Airways had in mind when picking me as a winner, but again, I didn't even have my first customer at the time.

It truly was a dream trip, and set me on a path with a business I grew for the next decade, which I ultimately sold when I felt like I'd outgrown my passion for it.

One thing I'll never outgrow, though, is my love of travel, and any chance I get to take free flights anywhere around the world.

Maverick on the Move

LGA TO MIA

New York, New York, to Miami, Florida
Shared by
Kelly Brownfield

*There are therapy dogs that people *claim are for therapy, where the owner just wants them to get a free ride, and there are THERAPY dogs, and Maverick is a THERAPY dog. In fact, the six-year-old gentle giant won an award as the 2023 American Humane Hero Dog. Part of his duties include offering comfort to military members and their families from across the country. The 150-pound European Blue Great Dane gently places a paw on the person he's trying to soothe, and it typically does the trick.*

Part of being there for others means having to board flights to get to them. Maverick and his owner, Kelly Brownfield, have been part of hundreds of special mission requests over the years, all over the country. As you can imagine, getting a pup the size of a person on a plane can be tricky, but it turns out with Maverick, what the airline is getting is a model passenger.

Maverick, shared by Kelly Brownfield

> *Typically, Maverick lays on the ground on a flight, but in this case, that wasn't possible with the seat swap, so the airline crew arranged for him to lay across a couple seats. However, when the flight attendants started their safety briefing before takeoff, Maverick sat at full attention, intensely watching the presentation. The entire plane was laughing, grabbing their phones out to record his reaction. Even the flight attendant was laughing hard, and gave kudos to Maverick for being his best passenger because he was actually listening!*

Maverick proved that with one recent flight on the way to Florida, as we learn here.

It was very late, and our seats were shuffled around. Typically, Maverick lays on the ground on a flight, but in this case, that wasn't possible with the seat swap, so the airline crew arranged for him to lay across a couple seats. However, when the flight attendants started their safety briefing before takeoff, Maverick sat at full attention, intensely watching the presentation. The entire plane was laughing, grabbing their phones out to record his reaction. Even the flight attendant was laughing hard, and gave kudos to Maverick for being his best passenger because he was actually listening!

And, you can bet, if there ever is an air emergency, it would be very comforting to have a therapy dog to help us get through it and be there for whatever the outcome.

The Demon Dog

JFK TO SFO TO RNO

New York City, New York, to
San Francisco, California, to Reno, Nevada, 2010
Written by
Brooke Siem

Some people can travel with their pets no problem. But their pets are not the so-called Demon Dog. Brooke's dog is, and she's the kind of animal not meant to fly. We know this from experience.

She looks cute, but she's named
Demon Dog for a reason

In 2009, I adopted a fourteen pound, street dog that earned the nickname "Demon Dog" thanks to her tendency to bite, snarl, and destroy. She lived with me in New York City, acting as my loyal, yet vicious security detail, but when I took a seasonal job at a winery on Long Island that wouldn't allow her to come with me, my mom in Reno, Nevada, agreed to take care of her for the six months that I'd be gone.

I knew the Demon Dog was going to be difficult on the flight, so upgraded to business class to give us more room, researched under-the-seat dog carriers and then spent the days leading up to the flight acclimating the dog to the carrier in my apartment. For insurance, I got some tranquilizers from my veterinarian (who protected himself with heavy rubber gloves whenever he treated her because had that bad of a reputation), but because the tranquilizers might upset her stomach, I was told not to muzzle her in case she threw up. Besides, the vet assured me, what he prescribed was strong enough to knock out a German Shepherd.

Days later, I thought back on the vet's inaccurate directive as my dog zig zagged up and down the aisle of my JFK to SFO flight. Pinned into my seat thanks to a beverage and culinary spread that had been placed on my tray minutes before, I saw the Demon Dog slither out from under the seat through a hole she'd apparently created in her "indestructible" carrier. The tranquilizer hadn't so much knocked her out as it had made her mad.

I heard screams and confusion from behind me and could tell exactly where the dog was on the plane, based on how far away the screams sounded. I worried she was going to bite someone, but luckily, she was drugged and confused enough to be picked up by a stranger, without incident.

A flight attendant cleared everything off my tray table and put the Demon Dog in my lap. She was supposed to go back in my carrier, but when I lifted it up, we could all see that it was missing an entire side. Rules are rules, the flight attendant said, so she brought me a pair of scissors and a roll of duct tape to patch the carrier back into working order.

I sat there, dog content and finally calmed down in my lap, surprised at the Terrorist Starter Kit the flight attendant had so nonchalantly given me. I figured the dog is far less of a liability on my lap than she is in the carrier, so I took as long as I possibly can to piece the carrier back together and tuck her away just before we land.

The story isn't over, though, because that same dog had to make the return trip on a flight six months later.

This time, I doubled down on the tranquilizer, filling a prescription designed for horses. I booked another set of business class seats, on a late flight for the short leg and a redeye for the long haul, hoping I could sneak her on my lap when everyone was sleeping, knowing she'd be cooperative as long as she was with me. I got a refund on my "indestructible" carrier and dropped hundreds of dollars on what I was told was a truly indestructible brand.

Except it was not. Again.

On my short flight from Reno to Salt Lake, the drugged-out dog broke out again. I caught her before she got away from my seat, explained to the flight attendant how sorry I was and asked her what in the hell I'm supposed to do.

The flight attendant said, "Is she a service dog?"

I was honest and admitted no, no she's not.

The flight attendant asked me again, *"Is she a service dog?"* I got the message and I said yes, she is a service dog. For the rest of the short flight, the Demon was calm in my lap.

Except the travel wasn't over and I still had a cross country red-eye to get through.

I marched straight to the counter for the next flight and explained to the airline worker what was happening with the Demon Dog and told him that if she could just stay in my lap, we wouldn't have a problem. He told me to hold her in the carrier for takeoff and landing, but that I could bring her onto my lap otherwise, as long as neither one of us made a fuss about it.

I figured he would be on the flight with us and would be able to support me if there was an issue, but not only was he not on the plane, he didn't communicate the situation to the flight attendant in my cabin. Even though all went well for the first hour—I refused any food, tucked away the dog under my blanket, waited for the cabin lights to go out—at some point, my dog's ear slipped out from under my blanket.

The flight attendant saw it before I did. She woke me up (and everyone else in the cabin), saying she had to go back in the carrier. I showed her the busted carrier and asked how she'd like me to handle this. The flight attendant didn't like that answer, ordered me not to argue, then called the captain—as if he wasn't occupied with, you know, flying the plane.

Completely devoid of context, the flight attendant told me the captain said the dog had to go under the carrier and that if I refused to cooperate, I could be put on a watch list. To which I laughed, because I had already done that! *(See the essay on Rushing the Restroom).*

She insisted I manually hold the dog in the carrier under the seat. For the next three hours. In the middle of the night. A stark contrast to the kindness of the flight attendant on the first leg and an example of why, even in the air, context is everything.

A Flight and a Show

Shared by
Pilot Simon Burke, England

Most of us board a flight with one mission: Getting from point A to point B.

But these days, that flight often comes with a show. And I'm not talking about the movies playing on the monitors on the seat back in front of you.

I'm talking about all the folks who seem to go a little crazy when they board a flight. Though it's still far from acceptable, it's becoming more and more common for passengers to get unruly. In fact, in 2021, there were reports of nearly 6,000 unruly passengers. That was the year masks were required on most flights, and many people didn't feel the need to follow that rule. The numbers have come down quite a bit since then, but still led to more than $8 million in fines passengers were charged in 2022. Just one fine can cost you up to $37,000, and the airline can charge you with more than one offense. Now THAT adds up to one expensive flight.

Ideally, everyone will behave and keep the crazy under control, because flight attendants are at the end of their rope dealing with it all. The issue has become enormous; 57% say a passenger has assaulted or harassed them in just the past year. That's more than half!

Just ask pilot Simon Burke, who is well-acquainted with wackos and wild people in the air.

My airline does what it can to make sure people who shouldn't fly never get to board the plane. But I recall one flight at an airport where many passengers are what we refer to as "well-heeled," which essentially means well-to-do, or more simply put, rich. And on this day, when passengers were boarding, one of the flight attendants mentioned a man was having a hard time finding his seat. She thought maybe he'd had a few drinks. I was busy with cockpit preflight duties, so I sent my co-pilot to go check on him. The co-pilot came back.

"Yep, he's wasted, alert security," he told me.

As the man who'd had a few too many was being escorted off the plane, I couldn't help but notice he seemed just fine to me, and maybe we were wrong to make him go. It bothered me a bit.

Until later, when I got the report on just how sideways things got once the man was back in the terminal.

"Did you hear what happened?", other airport buddies asked.

I told them no, and they went on to explain that the man went berserk as he was going through security. He literally got naked right there in front of everyone. Simply put, "He gave everyone a massive treat."

I'm not sure I would consider most of the outbursts a "massive treat", but it certainly does add another level of entertainment. Just cross your fingers it doesn't lead to your flight having to make an emergency landing, or re-routing somewhere no one intended to go. That just ends up with even more frustrated and potentially crazy passengers to contend with.

Side note: It's not a violation of the FAA to board your plane naked. It is, however, likely a violation of the airline's rules, so, well, keep your clothes on (literally)!

A Whole New World

FCO TO ATL

Rome, Italy, to Atlanta, Georgia, early 2000s
Shared by flight attendant
who asked to remain anonymous

There are a lot of things many of us take for granted.

Clean clothing. Running water for showers. Hygiene products to keep us smelling good. Heck, even food and eating utensils.

But not everyone around the world has access to these things.

It's not often that those same people who live without so much can board a plane and fly to another country.

But, after the war in Sudan, back in the days of George W. Bush's presidency, a special deal was arranged for many of the men who were "freedom fighters" to be rewarded with a flight to essentially start a new life in the U.S.

Imagine what that must have been like for them, to go from a world where basics didn't exist, then stepping into the technologically advanced world where you board an airplane in one country and land in another.

Well, my friend who worked as a flight attendant on one of those journeys can tell you, it was eye-opening.

It was eye-opening for the men and for us on the flight crew.

No one had told us in advance what these passengers, more than half on the plane that day, had been through.

But we figured it out quickly as these men from Africa, dressed in jogging suits or sweats, with an envelope hanging around their neck, walked onto the plane. We each wondered what the envelopes were all about, and had no idea what was in them.

What we did know was all 100 of these men seemed very out of place.

They had no luggage.

And few spoke English.

They had not bathed, and other passengers who weren't expecting to share a flight with the men were having a hard time tolerating the smell, so the flight had to be delayed while one of crew members ran to buy air freshener, hoping it would provide some relief.

And once we were in the air, things got even more interesting.

The men had no idea how to use the airplane bathroom.

When the food was served, they didn't know how to use the utensils. They'd never seen them in many cases.

When we walked by with trays of coffee, tea, or drinks, the special passengers were eager to try anything offered. Everything.

"Need sugar for your coffee, sir?", I'd ask. They'd take all 20 packets. They wanted to try it all, as much as possible.

My biggest memory was the man who, mid-flight, stood up and pulled down his pants, then proceeded to take off his prosthetic leg. I was stunned.

It's just not something I'd seen in all my years of working in the air.

We made it through the flight and found out later that inside those envelopes was essentially the money and directions to guide their new life in their new home country.

I have to admit, the entire experience was overwhelming for me.

And I'm sure it was incredibly overwhelming for the men, too.

How'd That Happen?

ATL TO FCO

Atlanta, Georgia, to Rome, Italy,
February 2022

When you have an overnight flight to Europe from the states, landing in a time zone six hours ahead of your own, it's important to sleep as much as you can to avoid jet lag and make sure you can hit the ground running.

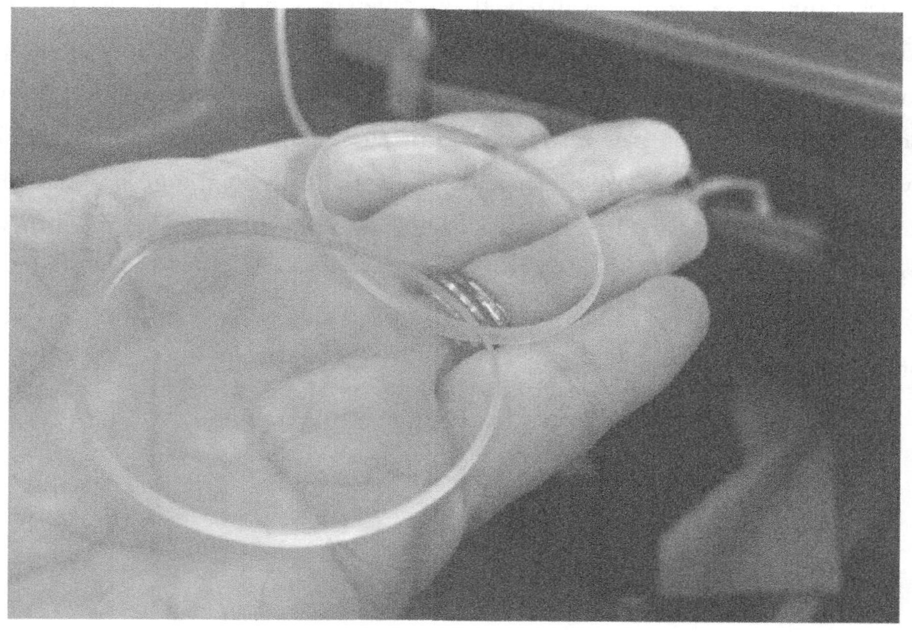

So, when my daughter and I were flying to Rome, Italy, we got settled into our seats, ate the meal they offered shortly after takeoff, and then cuddled up with each other as much as main cabin seats can allow. On this flight, that meant me leaning against the window seat and her lying across her aisle seat over onto my lap, to stretch out as much as her long body would allow. She wears glasses at night, so at some point, she put those in her sweatshirt pocket, pulled her hoodie over her head and passed out for the next several hours. The next morning, we woke up to daylight and the flight crew telling us to prepare for landing. We were excited to finally be getting to Italy, but there was a problem. Her glasses were no longer in her pocket. The assumption was they'd fallen out overnight, and most likely hit the floor. So we looked and looked, as much as we could in the tight space those seats allow, ultimately standing up, then crouching down in the aisle, thinking maybe they were under her seat somehow. But we didn't see them. What we did see were her lenses. No frames at all. Just two thick glass lenses (she's pretty blind without her glasses or contacts), sitting side by side. It was the oddest thing. Logic would say maybe they'd fallen into the plane aisle, and maybe someone had stepped on them, breaking the frames. Or maybe a crew member rolled over them with the beverage cart. But we asked and were told they knew nothing of the broken glasses. There was no note. And no frames. Like they'd evaporated magically overnight. Just two lenses sitting on the ground, tucked under her seat like some little eyeglass fairy had found them and set them there for safekeeping.

Fortunately, she travels with contacts and was able to wear them for the rest of the trip.

To this day, it's still not clear what became of the frames.

The Hide and Seek Passport

ATL TO SJU

Atlanta, Georgia, to
Costa Rica, October 2014

I was off to Costa Rica.

Pura vida.

That's the country's unofficial slogan. It means the "pure life" and essentially stands for the simple, joyful outlook they share.

I was almost on my way, but before boarding my flight, I got a message from the airline that I needed to show my passport to the gate agent. No big deal, I knew I'd need it when I landed and went through customs, so I whipped it out, showed it to the gal at the counter and waited to board.

Eventually, they started loading us up on the plane, so I walked down the aisle and found my seat. Someone was trying to get to their seat behind mine, so I hurriedly put my stuff away and settled in. I proceeded to make friends with the person sitting beside me, who happened to be going to the same event. We became fast friends, enjoyed a few drinks, and the flight flew by in no time.

Before we knew it, the flight attendants were handing out customs paperwork we needed to fill out before landing. One of the first questions it asks is for your passport number, and since I don't travel nearly enough to have it memorized, I went to pull out my passport book.

Only one problem.

I had no idea where I put it.

My mind was racing, trying to retrace my steps.

First, I checked the seat pocket. That's where my phone goes. And my water bottle. It would make sense my passport would be there, too, but it wasn't.

Then I pulled out my purse. That's a logical next storage spot. But nope. Not there, either.

Not in the backpack where I stored my laptop and camera.

And now I was starting to panic.

I was running out of places to look.

I told myself not to stress out, I had to have it to get on the flight so I must *still have it. Right?

That's what rational me was saying.

But anxiety-filled me was thinking I was never going to be able to get off the plane. They weren't going to let me into Costa Rica. The good vibes I was feeling on the flight were fading fast.

I spent 10 to 15 minutes going through everything again, thinking it couldn't magically disappear.

It could, of course, have fallen out of my bag at the gate, though. Or, it could have even fallen in that crazy crack between the gateway and the plane that you always have to step over, and when you do, you look down all the way to the tarmac, wondering if anything ever falls down there. Like a passport. That's probably where it was. Back in Atlanta, sitting on the tarmac. Useless.

My mind was spiraling, and the only thing left to check was my actual carry-on, in the overhead bin. Odds were pretty slim that I'd put it there, but I was out of options.

So, I stood up to pull it down, zip it open there in the airplane aisle, in front of everyone who already was thinking I was nuts at this point. And that's when the miracle happened.

I DID have my passport.

I was just sitting on it. All I had to do was stand up to find it!

And with that grand discovery, I was breathing a sigh of relief, once again embracing the pura vida!

Lost and Not Found

LGA TO CLT TO ATL

New York City, New York, to Charlotte, North Carolina, to Atlanta, Georgia, April 2013

As a TV news producer and travel reporter, I sometimes took trips for work, flying to and from destinations for stories, and my MacBook laptop was pretty much always glued to my side. I worked on flights, while everyone around me was relaxing, watching whatever show on their seatback screen, or scrolling away on their phone. Quite often, I'd download video from the camera I used for shooting interviews and then edit some of those clips on the plane, because that was something I could do without using airplane Wi-Fi.

For one trip, I traveled from my home in Atlanta, Georgia, up to New York and Connecticut, where I interviewed an airport manager about people abusing wheelchair service to skip security lines, etc. It was one of my favorite stories I'd produced in a while, so I was excited to get to work downloading the clips and starting on the script. On my way home, my flight was to go from New York to Atlanta, with a layover in Charlotte. When we got to Charlotte, I was so tied up with my story that I didn't even leave the plane during the layover. I worked straight up until they told us to put our devices away when we landed in Atlanta, so when they made that announcement, instead of putting the laptop away completely, I just slid it under the seat in front of me at the last minute, and started wrapping my head around getting out of the airport and making my hour-long drive home. It had been a very long day, and I was tired, my brain starting to feel a bit like mud.

So, once we landed, I grabbed my phone and carry-on suitcase from the overhead storage, then bolted off the plane, onto Atlanta's Plane Train (people mover between terminals), and out of the security area into the main airport.

And that's when it hit me.

I never got my MacBook laptop off the plane.

I guess at some point during landing, it slid up to the aisles in front of me, so I no longer saw it under the seat when I got up, and I was so focused on getting off the plane and going home that I totally forgot it.

I was in a panic. It had all of my interviews and video from the trip in a storage card on the device, and it hadn't been backed up yet in mid-air. I rushed back to the TSA line and was told there was no going through again without buying a new ticket. So I went to the desk for the airline I was flying (US Airways, which has since merged with American Airlines). They told me they weren't allowed to call the gate agent, to ask them to go look for it on the plane. They said my only option was to go to the airport lost and found. That was useless, since I knew it wasn't lost in the airport. It wasn't lost at all, in my mind. It was on the plane, on the floor, under the seat in front of me or a few seats in front of it, depending on how far it may have slid. They tried to tell me the cleaning crew would turn it in to lost and found, so I should at least file a report with them. I pretty much knew on the spot it was gone for good at that point.

And I wasn't wrong. Despite every attempt to locate it, through airline and airport forms, social media outreach, and more, it was just gone. It had a password you had to know to use it, so it was useless to anyone who found it, unless they just cleared it all out and started fresh, which ultimately is what I assume now happened.

I think I was more upset about all the video and images on the computer that I knew were gone forever than I was about the computer, which, for enough money, could be replaced easily.

The entire ordeal was gut-wrenching.

It turns out I'm far from alone in the grief of losing things on an airplane.

When I posted on social media about my misfortune, the large majority of friends who shared their stories of items left behind, from iPads to wallets to their kiddos' beloved toy, very, very few reported ever getting their items back. In fact, only two said their items were returned. Two out of about twenty.

So, my takeaway is listen when you're landing and the flight attendants remind you to grab everything you brought on the plane, checking seatback pockets, and the floor around you. Or, in my case, the floor on the seat in front of you, too.

A Final Flight

ATL

Atlanta, Georgia, August 2020
Shared by
Lori, Flight Attendant

When pilots retire, it's a big deal at Delta Air Lines.

They do a water cannon salute, have their family on board, and when you arrive back at the gate, there's a mini celebration at the gate area.

But, when COVID hit, a lot of the fanfare evaporated.

Entirely.

When I boarded my assigned flight in August 2020, I didn't even realize it was the captain's retirement flight. The First Officer mentioned it.

It was like a non-event.

And that didn't sit right with me.

Flights were limited, so there was no family with him. It was the height of COVID and there were only about 30 people on the plane. At the time, airlines weren't even able to offer service on the flight, meaning we weren't serving meals or even coffee or soda, just a water bottle and a snack. The planes were stripped down of supplies of everything but the minimum.

But I wanted to do SOMETHING.

So, recycling the paperwork we were given by the gate agents, we made him a sign, saying HAPPY RETIREMENT! Then we used band-aids to attach them to the plane wall and made an announcement as he made his final approach.

Sadly, no one could shake his hand or give him a hug to congratulate him on this massive accomplishment when he landed in Atlanta.

There was no one at the gate to meet him, no plaque that he'd otherwise be awarded.

As depressing as the situation was to me, I did what I could to make his landing for the last time at Delta's controls as memorable as possible, in a good way.

CHAPTER SIX

AFTER THE FLIGHT

You might think once you've gotten off the plane the adventure is over. Nope. Not always. Sometimes, there's much more fun to be had in the airport corridors. And sometimes, beyond.

The Fortunate Flyer

IAH TO LRD

Houston, Texas, to Laredo, Texas, 1991
Shared by
Ben A. (name requested withheld)

Ben may be one of the luckiest men alive.

Why?

Well, because the plane he was on, which had just dropped him off in Laredo, Texas, crashed on its very next flight, leaving Laredo.

I'll let him explain.

I was working in sales for an electronics company at the time. Part of my job involved traveling back and forth from Houston to Laredo, about 300 miles apart, a drive that could take six or more hours. So, it was typical for me to jump on a small, commercial plane flight between the two cities instead. On this particular day, I took the flight, got off, and then made the trip from the Laredo airport to my hotel, which took about an hour after collecting my luggage and getting a cab.

But by the time I walked into my hotel lobby, blaring on the TV screen was news of a plane crash, with video showing a massive black hole in the ground.

That's the image seared into my brain to this day.

It didn't take long for me to realize that was MY plane, the one that had just dropped me off, picked up about a dozen new passengers and headed back to Houston.

Only it never made it. 14 people on board died, including the crew.

Investigators talked with me about the crash a few weeks after it happened, trying to find out if I'd heard any noises, or felt any shakes, essentially asking if there was any sign at all that a crash was impending.

> "
>
> *But by the time I walked into my hotel lobby, blaring on the TV screen was news of a plane crash, with video showing a massive black hole in the ground.*
>
> *That's the image seared into my brain to this day.*
>
> *It didn't take long for me to realize that was MY plane, the one that had just dropped me off, picked up about a dozen new passengers and headed back to Houston.*
>
> "

I saw no indications of issues, and their investigation ultimately found there was a faulty part on the prop that the airline thought had been fixed, but ultimately wasn't.

The fact that the plane didn't crash during my flight was pure chance. Luck.

My wife, Leslie, to this day, gets emotional thinking about what could have happened all those years ago.

But personally, I feel safer on planes BECAUSE this happened.

After all, what are the odds I could be on TWO planes where a crash could happen?

My college statistics professor would argue the probability is the same, and being involved in one crash doesn't diminish your chance of being involved in another one. But I do like his optimism and would like to think I'd feel exactly the same way.

Blown Away

Maho Beach, St. Maarten, Princess Juliana International Airport, June 2017

Most people think of the beach as a serene spot, a peaceful place to let your worries fade away as you soak up the sun and play in the water. But if you're headed to Maho Beach on St. Maarten, an island east of Puerto Rico in the Caribbean, odds are you're looking for some exhilaration, too. That's because this beach is actually under an active runway for the Princess Juliana International Airport, which sees commercial flights, private jets, and other planes flying into and out of the airport on the island's Dutch side (St. Maarten is a country on the southern part, and the rest is Saint Martin, which is French). The island is a popular cruise ship stop, so many people will take cabs over to Maho Beach, specifically to see this stretch of land on the water where the planes fly so close to you that you almost feel like you can reach up and touch them. That's how I found myself there for this day in June 2017, with my family.

We met a taxi driver at our port and agreed on a price to drive us over to Maho. It's a trip that should only take about 20 minutes, though it may take much longer if other cruise passengers have the same idea and traffic gets backed up.

Once you get there, you'll see just how beautiful the beach is, with water you can see through, though it's just a narrow stretch of sand between the ocean and the road separating the beach from the airport. There are hotels, bars, and restaurants in this general area, where you can go to have lunch or drinks, or even stay overnight, and many have signs posting when various flights are scheduled to come in, so you know when to expect the next plane overhead. We particularly enjoyed Sunset Beach Bar, because if you get the right table, which is right outside, you can watch the planes landing while you're enjoying your meal.

Before we ate, we made our way to the water, where we chose to swim in the ocean, and were fascinated to see flights streak overhead while we floated, then splashed around in the surf. We then made our way up on the sand, where it's even more thrilling, because the planes appear to be skating right over your head. There were people around us who would duck down because it's so easy to believe they're coming in that low. There's not much of a landing strip (just a little over 7,000 feet), so pilots need to bring the planes as close to the beginning of the runway as possible for a smooth landing. As much fun as it is watching them from the sand, the best spot, in my opinion, is up on the road. It feels like you can literally air dry from the jet blasts when the huge planes take off. There's a fence separating the airport property from the road, but that's still not a totally safe distance. The power is so strong there are warning signs, letting you know it could literally blow you back into the ocean. I was worried enough that instead of watching from the middle, where we'd get the brunt of the blast, we stood off to the side in a safer zone, which was strong enough for me. I had my daughter grab on the fence, and then stood behind her and held on, too, just to make sure she wouldn't blow away. It's not something I'd suggest you try if you don't feel strong enough, and I'd definitely hold on, but our experience was thrilling.

If you love watching planes take off and land, I really can't think of a better place on Earth to do it.

A Trip to the Iceland Airport

KEF

Keflavik, Iceland, December 2022

What happens when you fly into a destination, only to find the airport is closed down, along with all the roads leaving that airport?

Chaos. That's what happens.

And frustration.

Then a bit of community.

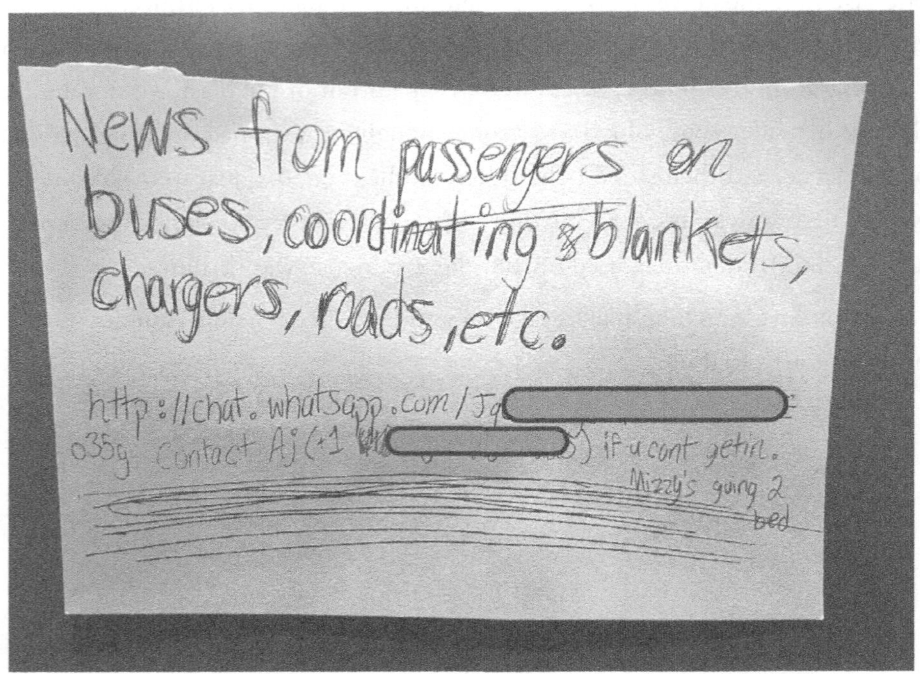

At least that was the case at the Keflavik International Airport when a blizzard hit the country in December of 2022.

Heavy snow and blizzards forced the complete closure of the biggest airport in the country, used for most international flights coming into and out of Iceland.

Sure, before the height of the storm, a few flights were able to actually land in the windy conditions, but once people got off those planes, they had nowhere to go.

Thousands of people ended up stuck. High winds and dangerous icy road conditions meant people couldn't leave the airport, and no one else trying to leave could get out.

For days.

Dozens of flights into and out of the nation had to be canceled.

About a thousand passengers were stuck at the airport for several nights. And they were NOT happy about it.

I was in Iceland at the time, trying to get TO the airport from the capital city of Reykjavik about 40 minutes away. It was disappointing enough not to be able to move about on the roads to take any planned excursions, or make it to our next hotel stay, but it was nowhere near as frustrating as what the people at the airport were going through, getting angrier by the day.

There was minimal access to food, and little to no communication from the airlines. At one point, one airline was able to book hotel rooms for many of the stranded passengers, but there was no way to get them to those rooms, with even the nearby access roads shut down. Once they did find some buses that could clear the icy roads, and many were told they'd be bussed to a nearby hotel, their agony was compounded when an overhead pipe burst and soaked all the cold travelers waiting for their escape.

It could have turned into a real apocalypse, but instead, ultimately, the passengers started to lean on each other, creating a barter system of sorts, with those who had food sharing with others, or exchanging it for the use of a portable battery to charge up their cell phone. They set up a WhatsApp number and posted signs to let people know where they might find a blanket, or to share updated information on roads and potential flights.

The floor was too cold to get any rest, so they made makeshift beds on luggage carousels, luggage carts, and even escalator steps.

Despite the brutal conditions they faced, they found a way to come together and try to make the most of a very bad situation.

Sadly, some people who'd planned and paid for a dream vacation in Iceland, where their return flights were within days of their arrival, never made it beyond the airport doors. Their entire vacation was summed up as a miserable visit to the Keflavik Airport.

Common Courtesy

DFW TO ATL

Dallas, Texas, to Atlanta, Georgia
Shared by
Marcia Wilson-Ahmad

Here's a lesson in always keeping your eyes open in the airport, even after your flight is done. You just never know who you'll bump into.

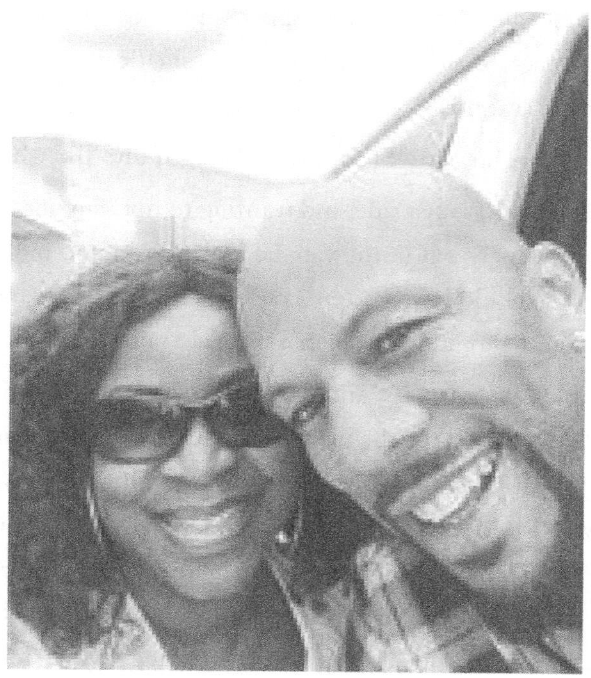

Marcia with Common

Growing up in NY, I've seen a lot of celebrities, so I'm somewhat jaded in that respect, and never want to come off like a "groupie".

There are very few people that would make me fan out.

Common (Aka Lonnie Rashid Lynn) would be in my top three.

I had just flown home to Atlanta from Dallas. I had been facilitating leadership training with store management teams. It was every day, all week, sun up to sun down.

I was beyond exhausted.

I was happy that I had made the decision not to drive home, and was waiting outside the exit for my son to pick me up. I was at the very first door, away from 80 percent of those waiting for pickups. I liked the calm and quiet of being away from the crowd. I noticed what looked like a white "church" van at the curb.

A few minutes later. My favorite rapper, and underrated actor *(see Hell on Wheels)* walks by me! I said "Hi, Common". I practically whispered it. I was surprised he turned around.

In the nicest tone, he said, "Hi, sis." He then got into the white van.

I was so bummed that my pride, and wanting to not "fan out," cost me a great picture opportunity. As he sat in the van, he looked over and must have seen me mouthing, "Darn, I should have gotten a pic". He motioned for me to come over. I said, "I was saying I should have taken a pic." He said, "Sure sis."

His incredible graciousness and kind warm nature felt like we weren't strangers at all. We chatted for the next 10 minutes or so, about music, Georgia, my son who I told him would have loved to meet him, as he was a rap music enthusiast, as well. I told him that he was on his way to pick me up. He said, "Is he almost here?" and looked at his watch. We chatted for another five minutes. I couldn't get my phone camera to work (probably nerves). He took my phone and snapped a selfie of us. He said, "It was so nice meeting you Marcia, sorry I didn't get to meet your son". He got in the van and the driver pulled off.

As he passed the more crowded area, I heard two girls screaming "Common, Common, OH MY GOD that's Common!" They then looked down the sidewalk and yelled down to me, "You were talking to him all that time, and you didn't even say anything?" As if I should have made an announcement and called them over.

My son thought it was cool that he was so gracious. It was nice to see and experience how humble he was.

Isn't it nice when your favorite celebs turn out to be even nicer than you thought they'd be?

The AirTag and the Missing Bag

As told by Elliott Sharod, "Avios Adventurer",
United Kingdom

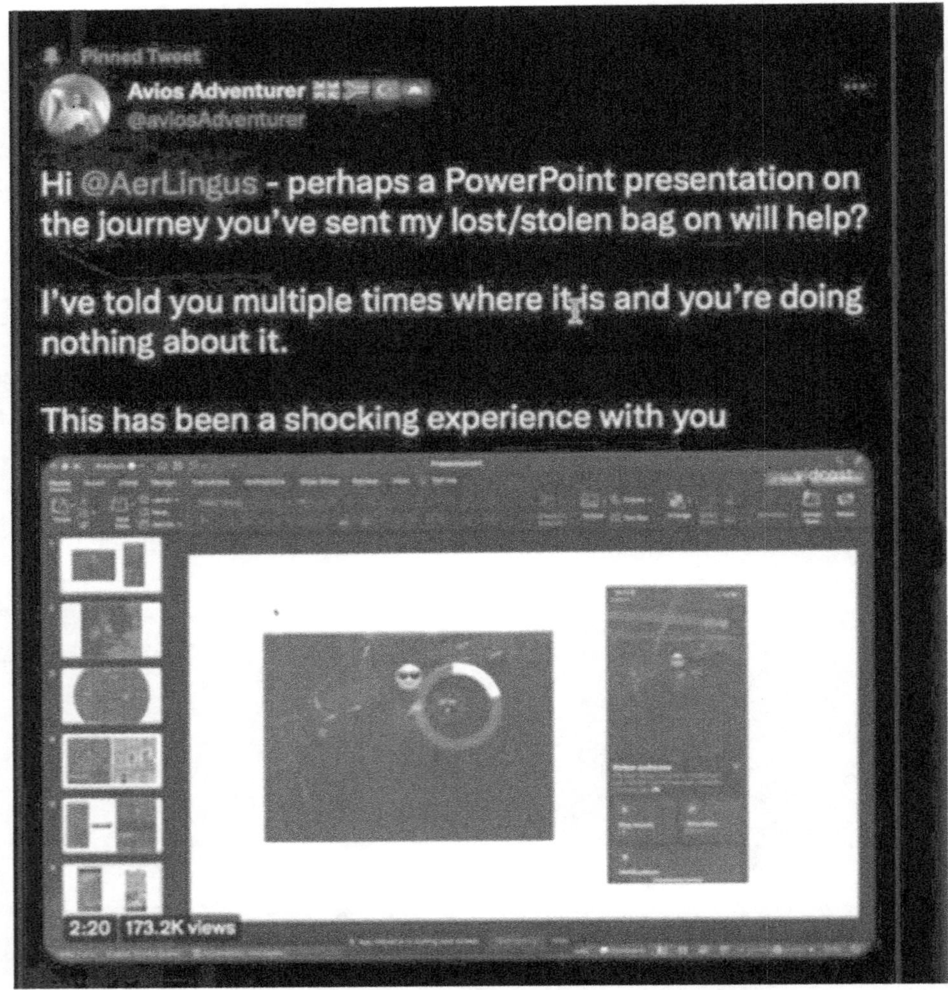

Odds are, if you travel often enough and check a bag, an airline has lost your luggage. At least for a day or two. It happens to the best of us. In fact, the latest statistics as this was written show that in 2022, out of the 470 million bags checked on U.S. carriers, six out of every 1,000 were mishandled, which means they were lost, damaged, delayed, or stolen (U.S. Bureau of Transportation). Sometimes, more often than not, the bag appears within days, and most airlines will deliver it to the address you share with them. But that doesn't always happen. And up until a few years ago, it was really hard to find that suitcase ever again.

However, with the advent of Apple AirTags, Tile Pro, and other Bluetooth tracking devices, it's a whole lot easier now. So, let's say your suitcase disappears and you can see it on your tracking app. But the airline, for whatever reason, still can't get it to you. Just how far would you go to get that suitcase back?

Well, if you're Elliott Sharod, of the United Kingdom, you'll go all the way to the address where it's located.

I didn't want to have to go on a crazy hunt for my luggage. I tried my hardest to convince the airline to handle things.

I even put together a PowerPoint Presentation and recorded videos that I posted on social media to motivate the airline to do more about my missing bag.

The bag disappeared when my new wife, Helen, and I were flying back home to the UK after our wedding in South Africa. When we landed, at first, three bags were gone, but we got two of the suitcases back quickly. The third one, however, which had some sentimental items from our wedding. And that one, when I checked my app for its location, showed up more than an hour away from us.

I reached out to the airline, calling, emailing, and messaging them on social media. I even reached out to the courier service that delivered the other two suitcases. But they were telling me the bag had been brought to my house, but they definitely weren't there. The airline's CEO's office told me their baggage team was investigating, but ultimately, it didn't show. And I could still see *exactly where it was.

Since I didn't think I was getting anywhere with the airline, I started using social media "to name and shame them."

Still, they didn't seem either willing or able to get the luggage back. And I could see it moving just a few streets away, which made me believe whoever now had it had no plans of giving it back. So, I called the police, considering it stolen. Again, that didn't seem to help.

So, I took matters into my own hands and made the drive with my wife to the address where the bags were last popping up on the tracker. Being so close, I was able to see it was in some kind of storage locker behind a building complex, locked. At this point, I called the police again, and since they now were concerned for my safety, they helped me get inside the locker, where we ultimately found other stolen things.

Finally, my bag was recovered, all thanks to the use of the AirTag (hidden in a sock in the suitcase) and a whole lot of persistence!

It's definitely wise to use a tracking device with your luggage, especially when checking your bags and going through multiple airports. That said, it can be risky to confront someone if you are able to locate a missing bag through the app. Things worked out well for Elliott, but be sure you evaluate the risk and reward if you end up in his shoes, and definitely call the police for help if you want to retrieve it. And by all means, always keep anything precious or priceless to you in your personal carry-on bag, which you know you won't be separated from.

Going the Extra Mile

DEN TO CLE

Denver, Colorado, to
Cleveland, Ohio, December 2016
Shared by
Kate Lacroix

On any given day, there are about a dozen organs, mostly kidneys, being transported by commercial airplanes to get to people desperately needing them to survive. It's necessary because, in most cases, the person donating a kidney is not in the same hospital, or even the same city, as the person on the receiving end. In 2016, Kate Lacroix was one of the people who stepped in to donate, giving up her organ to someone she never even met before. She did it to save a life. But, after the fact, she had a question for the airlines they hadn't dealt with before. We'll let her explain.

I had a therapist in college who helped me survive quite a few life events. So, when I saw years later, on social media, that she needed a kidney to survive, I knew I had to see if I was a match.

I went through the testing, and it turned out I wasn't HER match, but DID match another person on the kidney transplant list. So, even though my kidney wasn't going to her, it did initiate something called a donor chain, where another available kidney could save her life while I saved the life of a person I hadn't met. It's something that happens with a special algorithm and, in our case, was ultimately a 24-person chain that relied on organs being sent all over the country.

My kidney was transported by a commercial airline where I used reward miles, so after the dust settled from the transplant surgeries, I realized maybe I was eligible for some airline miles for that distance my kidney traveled. It added up to 1,333 miles, and if you like using your reward miles for free flights like I do, you know each mile can make a difference.

"

My kidney was transported by a commercial airline where I used reward miles, so after the dust settled from the transplant surgeries, I realized maybe I was eligible for some airline miles for that distance my kidney traveled. It added up to 1,333 miles, and if you like using your reward miles for free flights like I do, you know each mile can make a difference.

So, I thought I could ask the airline for the miles my kidney traveled...after all, it was a live organ. I mean, what rule says my entire body has to be on the plane?

"

So, I thought I could ask the airline for the miles my kidney traveled...after all, it was a live organ. I mean, what rule says my entire body has to be on the plane?

So, I asked. And was sent to a supervisor. They laughed and said it was a good question. And sent me to another supervisor. This went all the way up the chain, ultimately landing with the executive chairman, but his assistant said no.

I was happy to be part of this life saving surgery, but definitely disappointed by the airline's decision. I mean, if I could go the extra mile giving up a kidney, couldn't they go, or give, the extra mile, too?

I'm on Kate's side on this one. Pardon the pun, but imagine the miles the good PR could have gotten when her story was shared, and probably went viral. I can see it now: "KIDNEY SCORES REWARD POINTS!" This airline's motto is "More places. More miles. More adventures." This may have even led to "More Donors", which is really what it's all about anyway.

Angel in Disguise

BZE TO IND

Belize to Indianapolis, Indiana, 2011
Written by
Ginger Claremohr

When you're flying alone, it's pretty easy to juggle bags and navigate things on your own. Add a kid to the mix and it can be a lot. Add two kids to the mix and you're going to need a godsend to get through. Just ask Ginger Claremohr.

Leaving my kids' winter coats in the car made sense at the time. Our destination was sunny Belize, and when I made plans to take our two toddlers and tag along on my husband's month-long business trip, we were all supposed to return home together. So, he dropped us at the terminal entrance, I swiftly shoved the coats into the back seat, and he headed into the vast parking garage.

Unfortunately, he ended up having to stay in Belize for an extended period, so a month later, still in the dead of winter, I arrived back at the Indianapolis airport with two small children, two large bags, three carry-ons, and a useless stroller. And I had no idea where the car was parked.

I gave the kids their hooded beach towels for a bit of warmth, and tried to maneuver everything to the elevator.

It was fairly late for a weeknight at the airport, so the place was pretty dead. I figured I'd just take it slow and steady and pray the babies didn't suffer too much from the cold. As we approached the elevator, an old man with a luggage cart was coming out. He took a look at us and said, "Ma'am, do you need some help?"

Now, I have been in the Indianapolis airport at every time of day and night, and on every single day of the week, during every season of the year, and I have NEVER seen a luggage porter near baggage claim. Especially when the airport is pretty much closed for the night.

I replied, "Well, sir, I could use some help, but I have absolutely no cash on me right now, so I would not be able to offer a tip."

He kindly loaded up our luggage, which freed me to help the kids, and he took us all the way to the parking garage.

He was exceedingly patient while I located the car. I told him I would just set the suitcases on the ground so he could return to the terminal. Instead, he waited for me to take the kids' car seats out of the suitcase and put their coats on, and then loaded the luggage for me.

In ten minutes, we had done what would have taken at least a half hour of struggling by myself.

I had watched for an ATM, and then dug around in the car hoping to find tip money, but I had nothing.

I shook his hand and said, "I desperately wish I had something to give you, but may the Lord bless you greatly for your kindness tonight."

He replied, "The Lord blesses me every day! I was very happy to help you, ma'am."

And then he disappeared.

I was probably distracted by the kids and didn't see where he went. I thought I would wave goodbye as we pulled around and headed to the exit. But he was completely and utterly gone.

I believe God sent an angel in the form of an elderly luggage porter.

And that's the beauty of airports. There are wild, wacky, and wonderful things happening each and every day, all over the world. I guess this is our final nudge for you to be the good, and make someone else's trip to the airport better because you were there. In the end, you may never know the difference you'll make.

FLIGHT TO FREEDOM

KBP TO JFK

Kyiv, Ukraine, to New York, New York, December 3, 1999
Shared by
Anna Fishman

Sometimes, when you take a flight, there's no doubt in your mind it's going to change your life forever. That's something Anna Fishman realized as she planned to take a trip of a lifetime, back in 1999, and again, in 2022, when life came full circle for her, as you'll read here.

I grew up as a Jewish Russian in the Ukraine. There weren't many of us. After enduring decades of a communist dictatorship, many in the Jewish community emigrated in the late 1970s and 1980s. When I was 14 years old, my family was among them, as some of the last to leave in the late 90s.

It was 1999. My grandfather had secured a way for me, my parents, and him and my grandma to move to the United States, joining his brother and sister who had made a new life in America a few decades before. The deal with the visas was *he had to go, and we could join him. But without him, the U.S. was off-limits to us.

I knew how important this move was to my family, but it was still heart wrenching. I had spent my entire life in a teeny, tiny town of about eight-thousand people. To me, barely a teenager, who knew very little English, leaving my life behind in the Ukraine to go clear across the ocean to the massive metropolis of New York City was like moving from the moon to Earth.

We were only allowed to bring two bags per person. If it didn't fit in those two bags, we had to leave it behind. My grandparents sold their entire home for just three-thousand dollars. My parents gave up our home, too. We were literally starting over once we got to our new country with just $500 in cash for all five of us.

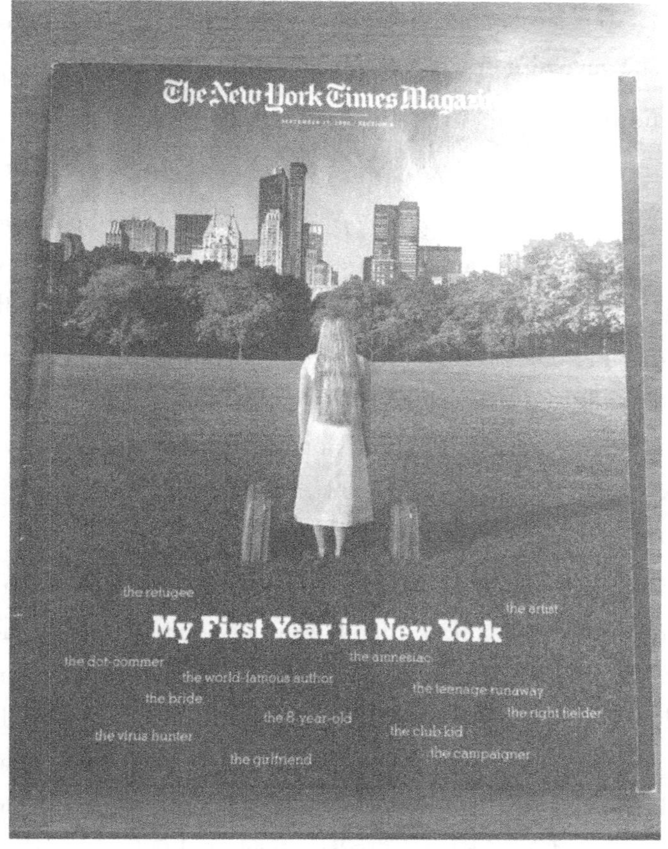

Anna on the cover of NYT Magazine, 2000

People fly all over the world each day, for all kinds of reasons. Often, it's just a fun vacation waiting at the destination. But sometimes, a whole new world is waiting.

And when the time came to go, we left our tiny town and took an overnight train to Kyiv, where we stayed at a hotel for the night. The next day, we had tickets to fly to America.

Everyone was stressed, and my grandparents already had medical issues; my grandfather had low blood pressure, and my grandmother had high blood pressure. Well, on the morning we were set to leave, my granddad's blood pressure spiked to dangerous levels. Since my grandmother had medication to bring *her levels down, she gave him one of her pills, trying to help.

Well, it didn't.

He collapsed, right there in the airport, an hour before our flight.

To this day, I remember him lying on the ground, foaming at the mouth. It was terrifying. Paramedics came and treated him, but there was no way he was making it on a flight. Which meant *we also weren't making it on a flight.

He was rushed to the hospital together with my grandma, where he stayed for a week. We didn't have a place to go at that point. We'd given up our homes. We really didn't have the money for a hotel for the next week. And we weren't even sure if we'd ever be able to get to America, since no one knew if my grandfather was going to survive at that point.

But he did, and while he healed, an old friend of my mother's let us sleep in her tiny home. She wasn't a close friend, even. Just someone she'd met on a trip years before. But this single mom fed us and cared for us in her home with her young daughter. She was truly a saint. She worked at the international school and I remember going to class that was taught fully in English with her daughter, just to sit in and help pass the time. It was so scary hearing this new language and it was just one class. I was about to make my whole life in America with a new language, new culture, and a new home.

Our previous plane tickets were useless now, so a refugee relief group helped collect the airfare money to get us all on a flight eventually. My grandparents were both 72 years old and I remember my grandmother was so worried about the flight that she kept saying that she would not make it, and we would have to bury her in the foreign land. But she made it! And so did my grandfather.

To be honest, we were all worried about the flight. It was my first time ever on a plane, and I will never forget the mixture of fear and excitement. Or how it felt when we finally landed at JFK airport, or the grueling hours we endured going through immigration.

After what seemed like forever, we got the green light and made our way to the home that had been set up for us. We were supposed to have arrived on Thanksgiving but didn't get on the flight until December third. When we opened the refrigerator at the new place, there was a piece of Thanksgiving turkey inside. Wild what you never forget, right? My room was on the third floor of this building, where the roof came together in an A, and there was a hole where I could see outside through the wall. Definitely different. And, as it turned out, not legal. After five months there, we were served papers telling us we had three days to get out.

Another relative of ours took us in. He was my uncle, someone my grandfather, at just 14 during World War II, had carried on his shoulders across much of Russia when he was just three years old, in order to save his life. All these years later, he hid us in his garage behind his house. But this wasn't allowed, and he was worried about nosey neighbors, so we had to stay in hiding, taping black garbage bags to the windows to block the light for several months.

But we survived it. The New York Times Magazine even published a story about our ordeal, not something I loved, because I already felt awkward enough at school, trying to fit in, barely speaking the language, without everyone knowing the details of my life. And then they even called and asked if I wanted to be on the cover of that magazine issue. This was my first year in NYC. They sent a cab to pick me up and my mom and I went to Central Park. They put me in a white dress and gave me two suitcases, setting up the picture with me on the great lawn and the city skyline in the background, taking photos at the sunrise. They even let me keep the dress. I thought I had won the lottery!

Now, two decades later, things are very different.

I'm married and have children, and a thriving business working in luxury travel. I plan very expensive trips for very wealthy people. And I fly quite a bit. Ironically, two years ago, as I was taking a flight on Emirates airlines. I never flew that airline before and I certainly never flew in business class, but I got a chance to upgrade to a business class seat, not for free, not for points, but for my hard earned money, which made all the difference in the world. I was invited to go to a prestigious conference in Italy and only a handful of American travel agents were invited on a fully hosted basis. But I wasn't worried about the conference, I was so worried about the etiquette in a business class seat. That good old imposter syndrome never fails! I boarded the plane and it felt like nearly everything was made of gold. I sat in my seat ready for takeoff, pulled out my phone and it hit me as I saw the date, that it was December third. The same date I'd taken that other flight, 23 years before.

I couldn't help but think back to teenage me, with only two bags to my name, full of terror. My whole life flew in front of my eyes as I was flying back across the ocean, this time on a trip to Italy for work. I was reliving all my experiences in life; gains, losses, all of it. And I was thinking of that woman who helped us when we were stuck in Kyiv, and her daughter. I knew I needed to reconnect with them again, and maybe find a way to thank them all these years later.

Sadly, the war in Ukraine had just started a few months before, so visiting them was not an option. My parents still kept in touch all those years later, so I reached out to them as soon as I could. The daughter had fled the country for Germany, with just a backpack. After some time, her mom came to visit her, and while there, was diagnosed with cancer. I sent them money to try to help, but the cancer ultimately took her life. Her daughter can't even collect her mother's ashes, though, because she doesn't have the proper papers. More collateral damage from the war.

My grandmother lived for eight years after our fateful first flight, ultimately passing away from a stroke. My grandfather made it more than two decades after the move to NYC, and would have lived even longer if depression from losing my grandma and COVID didn't take his life. They'd both survived World War II, and it's probably for the best that they now do NOT have to relive the pain of war in Ukraine all over again. I grew up hearing stories of them talking about the horrors of the Holocaust. Now I hear the bombing in the background when my family in America gets calls from loved ones we left in Ukraine two decades ago. And I think back to how close we came to never being able to leave, and just how different my life would have turned out. I do live the so-called "American dream", but still think of that life I left behind, and that pivotal plane flight that got me to my new home country.

Thanks for flying with us!

I have immense gratitude to each and every contributor who was willing to share their adventures with me in writing this book, and thank YOU for reading it. If you have a story that you think others will find fun, unexpected, or thoughtful, too, I'm collecting more for the sequel of this book, "More True Tales from the Terminal." I'd love to include you! Just send me an email to 101TalesfromtheTerminal@gmail.com

I also need to thank my boyfriend, Rob, who tolerated me talking about this book and all the stories in it ad nauseam. I'm also grateful for my crew of reviewers, Kimberly Shires, John Branning, Susan Kicak, and Kathleen Lopez Preston, for being willing to read through this book before I made it public. Thank you to Kathy Tully, who helped come up with the book name over a dinner during our first meeting, along with Kathleen, and all of the fabulous people I met at the Erma Bombeck Writers Workshop in 2022, which was the event I was headed to when this book idea hit. The incredible people who are part of that event cheer on each other's success, and that's everything to someone who needs a nudge making her dream a reality. And huge thanks to David Braughler, the publisher who just happened to be sitting next to me at the first breakfast of that event, and who, when I mentioned my book idea, told me, "If you write it, I'll publish it." Those seven words were my motivation for the next year as I put this book together.

Again, many, many thanks to the following people who allowed me to include them in this book. I can never tell you how thankful I am for you believing in me, trusting me with your story. To each of you, happy travels!

Tales from the Terminal Contributors

Rob Andres
David C. Baker
Tyler Beckley
Barbara Bellay
Ben A.
Kevin Benjamin
Rajean Blomquist
John Branning
Kelly Brownfield
Karen Bucci
Simon Burke
Oregon
Ginger Claremohr
Kate Clark
Tommy Clifford
James Coroy
Daniela Davenport
Lara and Marc DiPaola
Robin Dohrn-Simpson
Leslie Duffield
Richard Dunn
E.B.
Anna Fishman
Charles Harris
Rebecca Heiss, PhD
Joe Hernandez
Jan Hickel
William W. Hopper
Howard Kramer
Nirasha (Niri) Kumar
Kate Lacroix
Susan LaMotte
Paul Litwack
Emilie Lorditch
Steven Lowell
Todd Mazza
Keryn Means
Paula Miller
Lydia Langston Nall
Fadra Nally
Tanya Naphier
Shanon Pretorius
January Gordon Ornellas
Stacey Owens
Lisa Parker
Paya (from Prague)

Jennifer Rahaley

Lori Rea

Sharon and Kip Renaud

Michael Riordan

Peter Shankman

Elliott Sharod

Brooke Siem

Gloria Smith

Jonathan B. Smith

Susan Smith

Austin Stouffer

Katherine Terrell

Cindy Tutko

Eric Webber

Meredith Whitehead

Marcia Wilson-Ahmad

Meet Desiree Miller

Desiree is happiest when she's on another trip, or at least planning her next one. She loves traveling and meeting people around the world, seeing all the beautiful corners of the globe for herself. She's an award-winning freelance writer and former television news journalist, digital media producer, and blogger. She is the supervising field producer and writer for three travel shows and produces a weekly podcast with other travel friends called *Time to Talk Travel*. She also shares her adventures on multiple websites and television broadcasts, and now owns a company planning trips and retreats for others called Des Miller Travel Media. She had so much fun collecting and telling stories for this book, she's eager to write her sequel, and hopes you'll share your travel stories with her to be included in *More True Tales from the Terminal*.

Made in the USA
Middletown, DE
30 August 2024